FURY OF THE DRAGON

EDITORIAL

Welcome to "Eastern Heroes Bruce Lee Special" Volume 2 No. 1. In this issue, we delve deeper into Bruce Lee's iconic role as Kato in "The Green Hornet" TV series.

As many of our readers may recall, our last "Green Hornet Special" issue was one of the best-selling in the magazine's history. So, it is with great pleasure that we bring you an in-depth article by Chris Poggiali, film producer and author of the best-selling book "These Fists Break Bricks: How Kung Fu Movies Swept America and Changed the World." Chris Poggiali's article, "The Legacy of Bruce Lee's Ground-breaking Portrayal in the Green Hornet," provides a fascinating look into the lasting impact of Lee's portrayal of Kato on popular culture and the entertainment industry. Chris also offers an insightful look into the creation of the two "Green Hornet" movies. Additionally, we have a fantastic Bruce Lee column by Mike Nesbitt, featuring "The Robert Baker Letters," providing an intriguing glimpse into the relationship between two martial arts legends. For collectors, we have two great memorabilia sections, showcasing the many collectable items that were produced from "The Green Hornet" series. Contributors John Negron (USA) and Thomas Gross (Germany) showcase their collections, featuring many rare items that will delight any collector.
We would also like to make a special mention to J.J. Goodman, who passed away recently and was known worldwide by Bruce Lee fans for his collection and the restoration of the iconic car from the series, "The Black Beauty." This issue is a must-have for any Bruce Lee or "The Green Hornet" fan, so don't miss out on your chance to own a piece of martial arts history.

Once again thank you all who have supported the re-launch of Eastern Heroes and I look forward to producing another six issues over the next year.

Rick Baker

Rick Baker

Bruce Lee's portrayal of Kato in the Green Hornet television series is a role that has had a lasting impact on popular culture and the entertainment industry. Lee's performance as the Green Hornet's sidekick and driver introduced many people to the concept of martial arts and helped to popularize the discipline in the Western world.

Lee's portrayal of Kato was ground-breaking in many ways. For one, it was one of the first times that an Asian actor had been given a lead role on an American television series. This was a significant moment in the history of representation in media and helped to pave the way for future Asian actors to have more opportunities in Hollywood.

In addition to being a trailblazer for Asian actors, Lee's portrayal of Kato was also notable for the way it depicted martial arts. Prior to the Green Hornet, martial arts had been largely absent from mainstream American media. Lee's portrayal of Kato introduced many people to the discipline and demonstrated the athleticism, skill, and discipline required to master it.

One of the most memorable aspects of Lee's portrayal of Kato was the action scenes. Lee's martial arts skills were on full display as he fought off hordes of villains with lightning-fast moves and impressive

agility. These scenes were a far cry from the more choreographed and exaggerated fight sequences that were common in Hollywood at the time, and they helped to popularize the concept of "realistic" martial arts in media.

Despite being a sidekick, Kato was often the one doing most of the heavy lifting in the show. He was a crucial part of the Green Hornet's crime-fighting team and played a vital role in bringing down the villains. This depiction of a strong and capable Asian character was a refreshing change of pace from the typical stereotype of subservient and weak Asian characters that were common in media at the time.

In conclusion, Bruce Lee's portrayal

of Kato in the Green Hornet was a ground-breaking and influential role that had a lasting impact on popular culture and the entertainment industry. Lee's performance introduced many people to the concept of martial arts and helped to pave the way for greater representation of Asian actors in Hollywood. His action scenes and depiction of a strong and capable Asian character helped to popularize the idea of realistic martial arts in media and contributed to the evolution of the action genre.

HOW BRUCE GOT THE ROLE

In the late 1960s, American network television introduced a new program called "The Green Hornet." Based on a character that predated Batman by a few years, the original Green Hornet was a radio program that debuted in 1936. The TV version of the show was an attempt to capitalize on the popularity of Adam West's "Batman" series.
The program starred Grant Williams as

the Green Hornet, a crime-fighter who, assisted by Bruce Lee as his valet and sidekick, Kato (with a capital K), fought crime in a straight-forward manner. Williams was cast for his appearance rather than his acting abilities, and Lee, who was not yet a household name in America, was given the opportunity to showcase his martial arts and acting skills. Lee's role on "The Green Hornet" was a breakthrough for him, as it allowed him to demonstrate his charisma, athleticism, skill, and discipline on screen. His portrayal of Kato was so well-received that when the show was syndicated in Hong Kong, it was retitled "The Kato Show." In a crossover episode with "Batman," Kato was originally written to lose in a fight against Robin, but the scene was re-written so that they ended in a draw.

"The Green Hornet" was a TV program that aired in the late 1960s, based on a character that predated Batman. The show starred Grant Williams as the Green Hornet and Bruce Lee as his sidekick, Kato. The program was not as successful as the campy "Batman" series, but it did provide Bruce Lee with an opportunity to showcase his martial arts and acting abilities.

Bruce Lee as Kato...
ON THE BIG SCREEN

by Chris Poggiali

Anyone with an interest in martial arts movies knows that kung fu history was made on September 9, 1966 when American television audiences were introduced to a charismatic young actor in his prime time TV debut. The show was the 20th Century Fox production The Green Hornet and the exciting young actor was Bruce Lee, who played the titular crime fighter's sidekick and chauffeur, Kato. Much has been written about that series but very little has been documented regarding the two Green Hornet feature films that showed up in theaters following Lee's untimely death a half dozen years later.

I think about this as I emerge from the 72nd Street subway station and head toward Broadway. It's October 19th, 2013 – a sunny, seasonably cool Saturday – and I'm en route to a lunch meeting with Larry Joachim, the independent producer-distributor of two Bruce Lee "movies" that were compiled from episodes of The Green Hornet and shown in theaters all over the world. I've been corresponding with Larry and his son Marco for a year and a half, ever since they enlisted me as a researcher to help them track down the theater bookings and play dates for one of the kung fu movies they released through their Trans-Continental Film Corp., but this is the first time we've met in person.

I step inside the Viand Café and look around. Marco and I recognize each other from our respective Facebook pages, and he waves me over to a booth near the back. Larry, seated next to him, looks up from a menu and smiles widely as I approach. "Hiya, Chris!" he says, "You're just in time!" I exchange handshakes with father and son and sit down across from them. We order lunch, and then Larry shows me a folder of pressbooks, ad sheets and other promotional materials going back decades, mostly for children's films. After working as a standup comic and TV/radio personality, Larry co-produced the 20th Century Fox release Murder, Inc. (1960) and became a film distributor known as "the king of the kiddie matinees" in the New York City area during the 1960s and early '70s.

"I used to do one a month, in about 60 theaters," he explains. "Kiddie pictures, Saturday and Sunday afternoons. We always prayed for rain because we only had two days to make it. If it rained we would make money." One of his biggest successes came in 1967 with a re-release of

The Singing Princess, an Italian animated musical that had been dubbed into English in 1952 and features "the magic voice" of 16-year-old Julie Andrews on three songs.

Larry shows me an ad for the 5 Big Happenings of Horror, a spook show that promised appearances by Dracula and Frankenstein "in person" at each theater, which was one of his most popular matinees. "The kids tore down the theaters to get in!" he exclaims. "The ushers had to go up and down the aisles in the Frankenstein masks and Dracula costumes. There were 50 theaters in New York and New Jersey that played it. I remember trying to deliver the costumes in New Jersey the night before, and I didn't know any of the Jersey roads and I was hysterical, 'How am I ever going to get this stuff to the theaters?! Oh my God!' I went to one theater in Brooklyn – I'll never forget this. The line to get in was around the

block. This little kid came out of the theater and started yelling 'It's a fake! It's a fake! Don't go in, it's a fake!' I said, 'How much did you pay for the ticket? Here!' I gave him his money back and he said 'But it's still a fake!'"

Much of Larry's success during these years can be attributed to Marco, his son with Tony Award-winning actress Barbara Loden, who proved to be remarkably savvy when it came to the marketing of the matinees for kids. "When I was two years old, my father and mother got divorced and I moved in with my mother and [film and stage director] Elia Kazan," Marco says, "but I'd spend the weekends with my dad, who was around the block – 68th Street, 69th Street in New York – and was doing the kiddie matinees at the time. He would ask me questions and listen to my suggestions because I was a kid and he figured I knew what would appeal to other kids."

He cites an example in which Larry overheard a long, enthusiastic conversation between Marco and his friends about the Haunted Mansion, the popular E ticket attraction at Disneyland in California and the Magic Kingdom in Florida. "This was the early '70s so [the Haunted Mansion] hadn't been open very long," Marco recalls. "It was still new and exciting. My dad was listening to us, and he asked me later 'Would you like to see a movie of the Haunted Mansion?' I said 'Yeah, sure!'" In October 1973, Larry ran a kiddie matinee called Haunted Mansion, which turned out to be Who Killed Doc Robbin? (1948), the second of two attempts by Hal Roach and Robert F. McGowan to

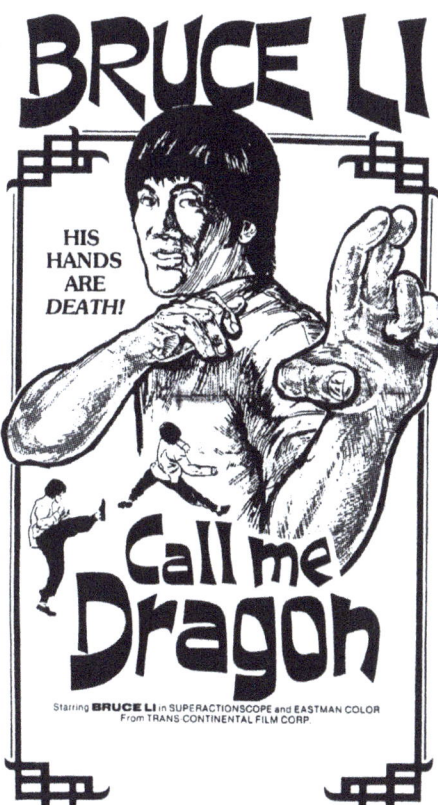

revive their Our Gang comedies as 55-minute color b-features. Marco smiles at the recollection. "It wasn't the Disney Haunted Mansion, but it was still fun."

Just as kung fu fever was beginning to hit the United States, ten-year-old Marco saw a television ad for Five Fingers of Death and insisted his dad take him to see it. Larry covered Marco's eyes every time the blood flew onscreen, but Marco fell in love with kung fu and that led to an obsession with Bruce Lee. Not long after Lee's death, Marco remembered that Larry had rented the 1966 Batman movie from Fox a couple of years earlier for a very profitable weekend of matinees. "I told my dad that the producer of Batman had done another show, The Green Hornet, that Bruce Lee was in, and if he could buy that series we could make it into a movie. He didn't think he could get the rights, but I kept saying 'We can really make a lot of money.'" Larry was a divorced dad running a business on tight margins, so the cash flow would sometimes slow to a trickle. "I was always worried about my father," Marco admits. "He was always hustling."

Larry still had connections at Fox because of Murder, Inc., and his former agent, Maurice Morton, was now the vice president of administration at the studio, so it was worth a shot. After a few calls Larry flew to LA and met with

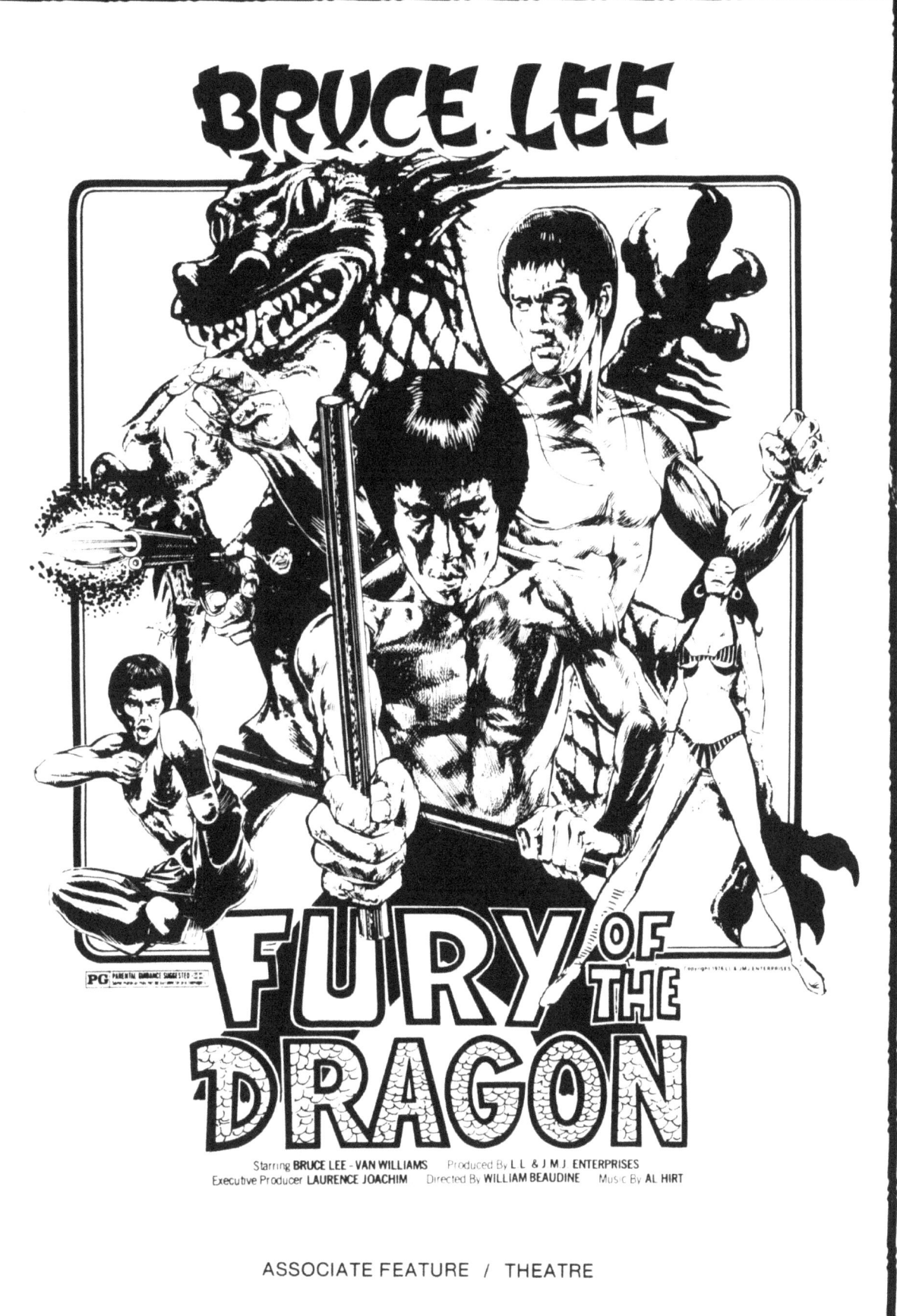

the appropriate Fox executives, who had no idea what this east coast crackpot distributor saw in a seven-year-old, one season wonder, but were willing to take five thousand dollars off his hands for the U.S. theatrical rights. Larry smartly offered them another ten grand for the world rights, and they went for it.

Back in Manhattan, episodes of The Green Hornet began arriving from Fox on 16mm reels, three or four a week. Larry wasn't sure how to get started so he turned the project over to Marco, who took detailed notes while watching all of the episodes and selected the ones he thought would work best: "The Hunters and the Hunted," the two-part "Invasion from Outer Space," and "The Preying Mantis." He then brought the reels to Kazan's brownstone and started cutting them up on the same equipment that was used to edit his mom's acclaimed film Wanda (1970). Larry was there with Marco for most of the editing. "My father helped – we did it together," Marco stresses, "but I was basically the one doing it because he didn't know. His attitude was, 'Whatever you like, the other kids will like!'"

After watching the rough assembly, Marco decided there wasn't enough fighting in this new Bruce Lee movie he was creating, so he consulted his notes to find similar fisticuffs he could use to extend these sequences. Larry thought it wouldn't make sense if they inserted other fight scenes, but they did it anyway, cutting in material from seven additional episodes including a scene from "Beautiful Dreamer, Part 2" simply because it shows Kato throwing one fast punch that knocks somebody out cold. Who would care, or even notice, that the whole point of the scene is a racetrack robbery that has nothing to do with the other three plotlines? Audiences just wanted to see Bruce Lee in action.

"When we were finished, it was this whole jumble," Marco confesses. "My dad sent it back to Fox, and they edited it, made a master negative and fixed it up a bit, because obviously we weren't editors. Music was jumping in and out and all sorts of stuff was going on. If you watch it today, you can see that it's edited a little strangely."

Next, Larry and Marco turned their

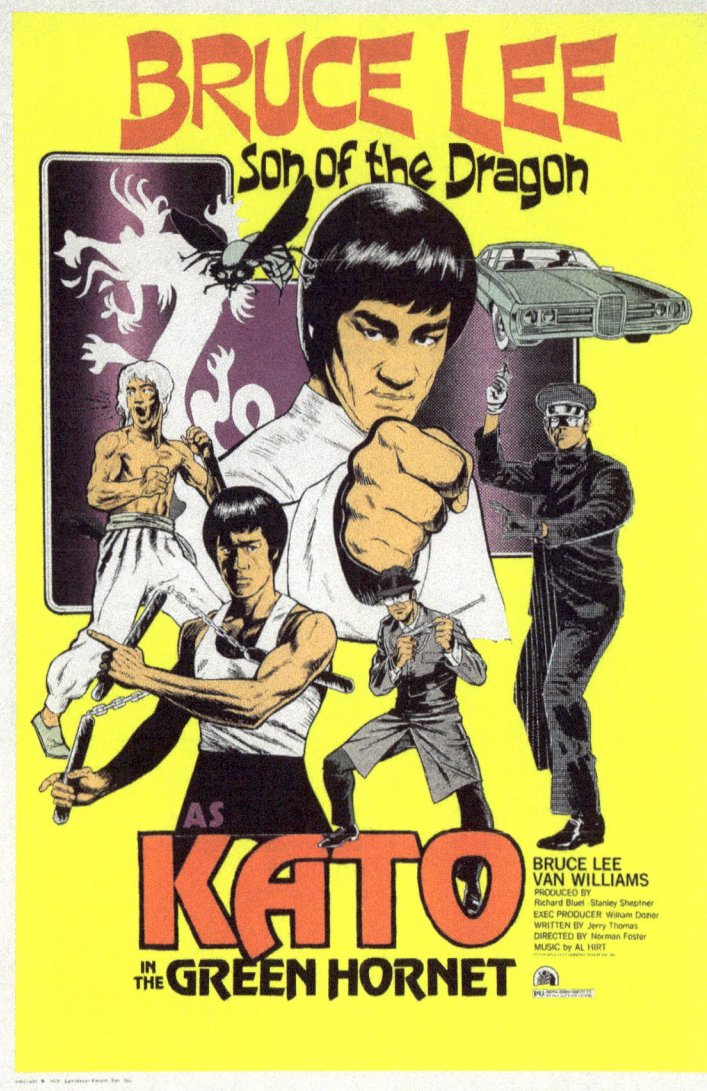

attention to the advertising campaign. The posters were already printed and ready to ship, but Marco was having doubts that the artwork – by a New York Times fashion artist – would appeal to the kung fu crowd. He had seen comic book artist Jim Janes' rendering of Bruce Lee on the cover of The Monster Times #32 (April 1974) and convinced Larry to hire the newspaper's designers, Larry Brill and Les Waldstein, to create a new poster design using art by Janes. Father and son then worked together with scissors and glue to put together full-page ads for Boxoffice and Variety.

When the film came back from Fox in cleaned-up 35mm, Larry screened it for friends and family – and the reaction when the lights came up was anything but encouraging. "Nobody liked it," Larry recalls. "I had a guy working for me, Ray Wells – he said, 'This isn't even good enough to sell as a kiddie matinee!'"

"They all kind of said 'This isn't a good film' and put it down," Marco remembers. "It was very upsetting, because my dad had basically put this whole thing together based on me saying that Bruce Lee was my favorite movie star and the picture would make money." But Marco's faith never wavered, and he told his dad, "Don't worry, it's great. I love it."

Larry could be a very funny guy, but he was definitely no fool, especially when it came to business. He understood how Variety compiled their 50 Top-Grossing Film chart every week: it was a sample of roughly 700 theaters in 20-24 cities

and represented only 7% of the overall number of cinemas, both hardtops and drive-ins, in the U.S. Therefore, one strategically placed 35mm print could conceivably land a film mid-way up the chart, proving its profitability to exhibitors who might otherwise be wary of booking a seven-year-old failed TV series as a first-run feature. Larry ordered two 35mm prints from the lab and zeroed in on Chicago and Philadelphia as his first targets, since Bruce Lee was a big box-office draw in both cities.

Tales of the Green Hornet premiered at the Oriental Theatre in the Chicago Loop on October 18, 1974. The admission price was $3.00, which is about $18.00 today when adjusted for inflation. Free Bruce Lee posters were given out to the first 2000 patrons, which helped attract crowds, and the gamble paid off. The film grossed $45,000 in five days, earning it the #28 position on the Variety chart.

The following Wednesday, under a shortened title and with "the original 7 minute screen test of Bruce Lee" screened first as a bonus attraction, The Green Hornet opened at the Fox Theater in Philadelphia. The City of Brotherly Love responded lovingly, and by the end of the third week the film was still on the chart and boasting a total gross of over $120,000 from just the two theaters. Today, that's roughly $725,000.

Three more prints were struck and the Hornet's next landing was at two theaters in Detroit (the Palms and the Mercury) and one in Boston (the Astor) on November 13, 1974. The Motor City was a crapshoot since it was one of the few areas in the country where people could literally stay home and watch The Green Hornet for free (WXON-TV had been airing episodes for nine months). Still, this was an opportunity to see Bruce Lee commercial-free and on a big screen. The Mercury Theater alone reported $14,000 for the week – not bad, all things told.

With the money he'd made so far, plus a good chunk he borrowed from his mother, Larry ordered 100 more prints. On November 27 – the day before Thanksgiving – The Green Hornet opened concurrently in the New York tri-state area, Cincinnati, Sacramento, Salinas, and the San Francisco Bay Area. The five boroughs of New York accounted for 40 of those prints. On opening day, Larry and Marco went downtown to watch the movie with a Times Square audience. "As we approached 42nd Street, we noticed a line that went around the block," Marco remembers. "I said to my dad, 'That can't be the line for this film!' He said, 'I don't know. Let's see.' We got closer and sure enough, the line started at the [New Amsterdam Theater] box-office and went around the corner, and it was for The Green Hornet. We went inside and it was standing room only. People were cheering. It was incredible. It was like we had hit the lottery."

By now, Larry's phone was ringing off the hook. He'd sometimes have two calls going at once, with a receiver in each ear – "You want Bruce Lee?" he'd ask one theater owner and "Yeah, we got The Green Hornet!" he'd answer the other. His assistant, Ray Wells, was fluent in Spanish (his real name was Raphael Arguelles) and had managed a Spanish-language movie theater in New York. Because of this, and coupled with the fact that Larry owned the worldwide theatrical rights to The Green Hornet,

Wells was sent to South America to shop the film around country by country. "First time he called me – 'I got an offer here, Larry. It's ten thousand dollars for Venezuela, and it's a great offer! You're never gonna get a better offer!' I said 'Ray, shut your fuckin' mouth! Come back here to New York right now! I'm not using you anymore!' [Pause] 'Well, let me talk to the guy again.' So he called me a day later – 'He's up to twelve thousand.' I said, 'Fuck you!' Next day it's 'OK, I got you twenty-five thousand.' I said, 'I'll take it!' Every single country in South America we went through just like that."

The movie made a mint, and Fox – still baffled by its success – agreed to a sequel. Larry was hesitant at first, believing they had already mined all the best material from the series, but Marco checked his notes and assured him there was still a lot of cool stuff left to justify a second trip to the well. As before, Marco selected the four primary episodes first –"Trouble for Prince Charming," "Bad Bet on a 459-Silent," "The Ray is for Killing," and "The Secret of the Sally Bell" – and then started looking at others to find fights and interesting moments he could splice into the main narratives.

Meanwhile, the box-office success of The Green Hornet enabled Larry to produce his own martial arts epic, Black Samurai (1976), and start importing Asian action movies for theatrical distribution through his new company, Trans-Continental Film Corp. One of the first movies he planned to acquire was Call Me Dragon (1974), starring Siu-Lung Leung (Bruce Liang) and Yasuaki Kurata, but just as he was about to make an offer for the film, he caught wind of a more pressing issue: a movie titled Bruce Lee Against Supermen had opened in Guam, with newspaper ads that depicted Bruce Li (Taiwanese actor Ho Chung-tao) dressed as Kato and the tag line "Can the Green Hornet's fantastic kung fu defeat the magical tricks of the supermen?!" Larry was furious. He and Marco had just started working on their Green Hornet sequel, and the last thing they needed was a copycat movie beating it to U.S. theaters and potentially jeopardizing the deal with Fox. "This guy, Jimmy Shaw, made a complete Green Hornet picture in Taiwan and he had Bruce Li in it!" Larry says. "He stole the whole picture! I said 'You can't do that!' He said 'Oh yes I can!'"

Larry's solution was to buy the movie outright from Shaw and then sit on it, but while closing that deal he lost Call Me Dragon to another buyer. That's when Larry realized what he really liked most about Call Me Dragon was the title, and because titles don't fall under copyright protection, what was stopping him from taking it and sticking it on some other movie – like, perhaps, the piece of junk he'd just purchased from Jimmy Shaw? Absolutely nothing, and so that's what he did. Trans-Continental released Bruce Lee Against Supermen in New York on November 17, 1978 under the title Call Me Dragon, with nothing in the trailers or print ads suggesting the movie had anything to do with Kato or the Green Hornet (As for the real Call Me Dragon, that finally arrived in U.S. cinemas in 1982, from another distributor, as Fighting Dragon vs. The Deadly Tiger).

As for the Green Hornet sequel, Marco ended up pulling scenes from twelve additional episodes to create Fury of the Dragon (1976), an even crazier concoction than the first movie. Barely three minutes in, footage of an airport fight from "Dateline for Death" is interspersed with different villains fighting at some other airport from "Trouble for Prince Charming." An hour later, in the middle of "May the Best Man Lose," Marco cuts

to a scene in which Britt Reid and Kato listen to a recording of someone named Mr. Tubbs being shot, but viewers have no idea who Mr. Tubbs is because this scene was also pulled from "Dateline for Death," with little or no regard for continuity. "I felt there wasn't enough of Kato without his mask on," Marco explains, "and since you get to see Bruce Lee's face in that scene I wanted to put it in the movie someplace, so I just stuck it in there." There's also a different (and deceptive) opening credit sequence in which the show's theme song – Al Hirt's memorable take on "Flight of the Bumblebee" – is replaced by Keith Mansfield's "Aggressive Jazz Theme" from the 1968 KPM Music Recorded Library LP Flamboyant Themes. In addition, Bruce Lee receives top billing, series star Van Williams isn't credited at all, and executive producer William Dozier's name is dropped in favor of production credits for Larry and Marco. William Beaudine, who died in 1970, receives top directorial credit.

Fury of the Dragon premiered in New York on November 24, 1976 with the Bruce Lee screen test as an added attraction and a limited edition Bruce Lee newspaper designed by Brill-Waldstein given out to patrons. Larry changed the title to The Green Hornet II: Kato's Revenge for some bookings the following year, on a double bill with a kid-friendly cut of Black Samurai. In fact, both of the Green Hornet movies were repackaged several times and remained in theatrical release into the 1980s. Bryanston Releasing made a deal with Larry to run The Green Hornet as a co-feature with Return of the Dragon in New York on

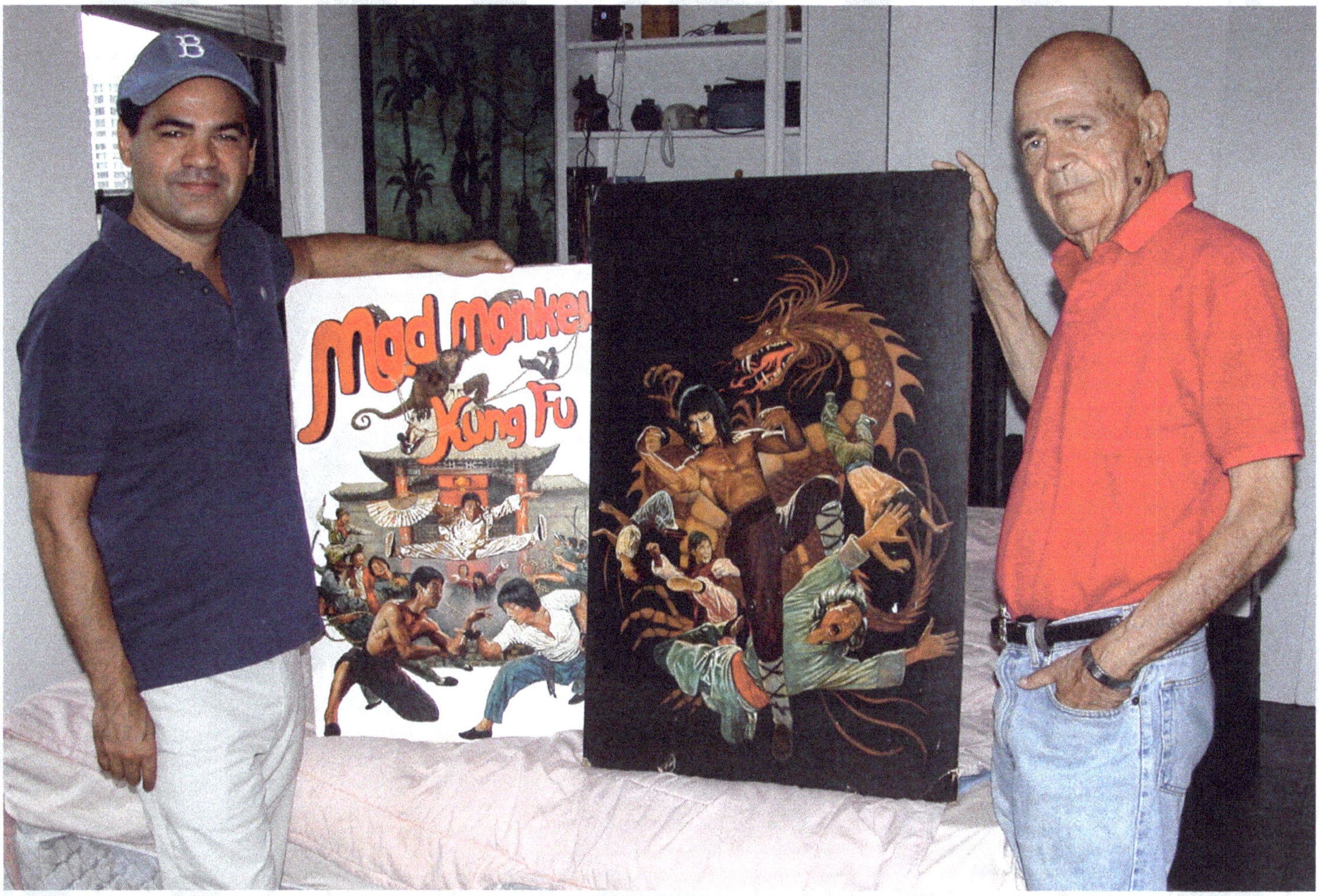

CONTACT Larry Joachim
TEL. [212] 724-7473
[212] 873-5874
48 West 69 St.
New York, N.Y. 10023

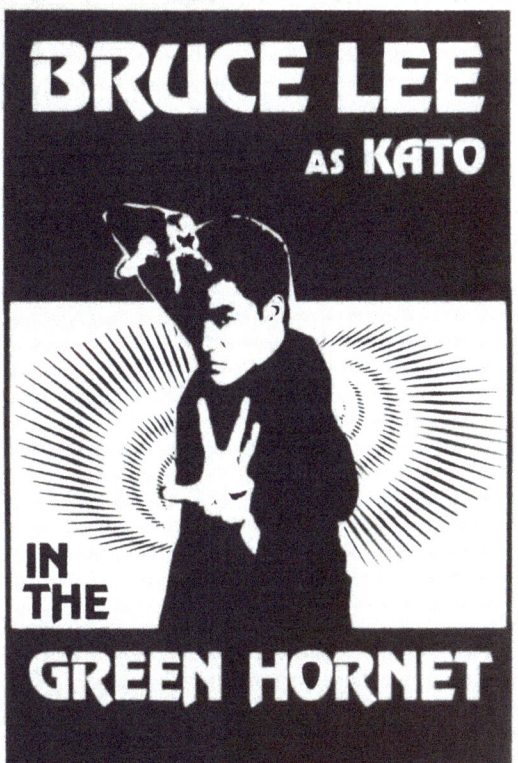

September 12, 1975. Simpson's Distributing Corp., a sub-distributor based in Charlotte, rented 50 prints of The Green Hornet and paired them with Godzilla vs. The Bionic Monster for a "Bruce Lee and Godzilla" double bill that was booked throughout the Carolinas in May 1977. When Columbia re-released the Bruce Lee movies in the early '80s, they sub-licensed The Green Hornet to run with Fists of Fury on a double bill that opened in the New York City area on November 6, 1981. Eight months later they made another deal with Larry for Fury of the Dragon and Black Samurai to fill out a "Kung Fu Triple Threat" program with Return of the Dragon that played in a dozen New York theaters the week of August 6, 1982.

Today, Marco's Green Hornet movies have fallen into almost total obscurity. As of this article's writing there's no mention of them on Wikipedia, even under the entry for the television series. That's a shame, because they're not only two of the most financially successful 'Bruceploitation' movies, they're the only ones to star the real Bruce Lee without using body doubles or imitators. More importantly, the two films were created by a pre-teen and deserve recognition as the earliest and most widely seen and distributed examples of what is now called a "fan edit."

AUTHOR'S NOTE: Larry passed away in Beverly Hills on November 17th, 2013, less than a month after our lunch meeting at Viand Café. The headline of his Variety obituary reads "Larry Joachim, Distributor of Kung Fu Films, Dies at 88."

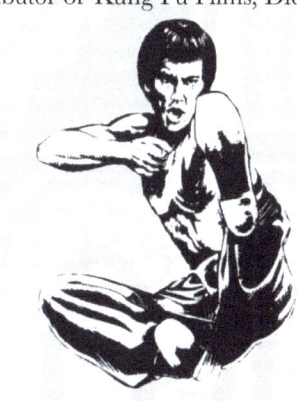

THE BRUCE LEE COLUMN
THE ROBERT BAKER LETTERS
By Michael Nesbitt

On July 16, 2021, the Bruce Lee community was in disbelief when Heritage Auctions held an auction for a collection of 51 letters belonging to the late Robert Baker. Robert, a practitioner in martial arts, was a student and close friend of Bruce Lee's, who also at times, acted as his bodyguard. But it is for his portrayal as Petrov, the Russian bad guy in Bruce Lee's Fist of Fury, that he is most known for. Robert was somewhat of an introvert, and shunned the limelight, very rarely making public appearances. One of the only appearances he made, and possibly his last, was at the Tracking the Dragon Convention organised by Chris Alexis in 1990. Unfortunately, Robert died of cancer three years later in 1993. Only a small number of long-time Bruce Lee experts knew of the existence of the Robert Baker letters, and since the letters were written during the late 1960s, and early 1970s, they had never seen the light of day, maybe because of their controversial content. Other items from the Robert Baker auction, included a 1st edition copy of Bruce Lee's book, Chinese Gung Fu; several behind-the-scenes photos from Fist of Fury; an exercise book with handwritten notes by Robert detailing his experiences while making Fist of Fury; and an invitation from Golden Harvest for a dinner in honour of Robert. The whole collection of items from the Robert Baker auction sold for around $160,000. When Robert passed away his widow packed all of the items up and stored them in her garage, where they stayed for the next twenty-eight years.

Forty-three of the letters were written by Bruce Lee to Robert, and the other eight letters were written by Linda Lee, Bruce's wife. What shocked most of the Bruce Lee community, was the unknown existence of these letters, and more importantly, and historically, the content written between the two friends. Basically, the content of the letters showed that Bruce Lee not only partook in the taking of drugs, but he also sold drugs and even was somewhat of a drug smuggler. Reading this, it would be safe to say that most Bruce Lee fans would be shouting out; "what a load of rubbish!" However, the content of the letters and their authenticity have never, or could ever be in dispute. I think to most long-term Bruce Lee collectors, these revelations came as no surprise, however, the graphic and candid nature of the letters, left even the hardened Bruce Lee fan in disbelief.

The letters start off very friendly, with the earliest one dated the 26th of December 1967, in which Bruce tells Robert to contact Allen Joe and figure out ideas on how to get James Lee to a surprise birthday party (1). In another early letter, dated the 1st of April 1969, Bruce mentions to Robert about some training footage they had taken, which he was going to send to Black Belt magazine, his future travel plans and Bruce getting over some illness, maybe relating to his back problems. The first letter we get that indicates anything relating to drugs, is a short letter dated December 12, 1969, a letter I personally was able to win at the auction, in which Bruce thanked Robert for bringing him "the stuffs? especially a pipe and painting," (2). If it wasn't for the other letters in the collection, this comment could easily be passed off, but considering what was to come, the words "stuffs" and "pipe" certainly indicate something more nefarious. The next letter, dated February 2, 1970, goes a little bit further and thanked Robert again, this time for; this "holy stuff," (3). Holy Stuff or Holy Grail was often a reference to Marijuana.

In a letter dated March 6, 1970, Bruce talks about returning from a European trip, where he visited both Switzerland and London, this is very interesting considering a lot of so-called Bruce Lee experts claimed that Bruce never visited England. He also thanks Robert for the papers he sent him before his departure; Bob had worked in a paper factory and would supply Bruce with the writing paper and envelopes with his headed Jeet Kune Do symbol on them. The letter signs off; "by the way, wouldn't mind going in with you for some of this "holy stuff" before leaving for H.K," (4). In a letter dated March 11, 1970, Bruce writes:

"I'm planning to leave for H.K. on April 1st, and definitely would like to store up on some "Holy stuff" to bring over there. See if you can come up with something good." Bruce then goes on to say: "The paper that I had taste kind of sweet and that definitely adds to it. So see if you can get some "good tasting paper," (5). On June 17, 1970, Bruce stated in a letter: "I told Linda to call you to forget about the "stuff" because I really don't need them in my training. I feel that I have "gained" in trying them, but excessive indulgence of them just isn't in my road in Jeet Kune Do," (6). Most people think he may be talking about steroids, something he may have initially taken for the severe back pain he suffered.

In one of the most revealing letters dated June 22 1971, it looked like Bruce may have been organising a secret getaway with a mistress, in it, he states: "I plan to come up — depending when I finished shooting — from July 2 (friday nite) to probably Tues or Wed (7). One thought here: I "might" come up (fly) with Teresa and she probably stays Friday nite (July 2), Sat nite (July 3) and leave Sunday (July 4) afternoon

or so. The question is, is it convenient for Bev and the kids to spend Friday nite, Sat. and Sunday morning at her mother or somewhere and make up some convenient jazz, for I don't want Bev to know about this. Of course it has to be convenient or else forget it. My mother and everybody is at my house now. Let me know, and remember if only it is convenient and flow and everything is cool." (7).

Even when Bruce was in Thailand filming his first major movie, The Big Boss, he kept in regular contact with Robert Baker, and in a letter dated August 3, 1971, he claims: "Thailand is full of G but I have

Bob,

I'm planning to leave for H.K. on April 1st, and definitely would like to store up on some "Holy stuff" to bring over there. See if you can come up with something good.

Am working on the story Mon., Wed., and Fri., 4 to 6 with Coburn and Silliphant, making good progress.

The paper that I had "taste" kind of sweet and that definitely adds to it. So see if you can get some "good tasting" paper.

Take Care

Bruce

very little time for it though. I have to say it is "extremely" good." (8). The G stands for Ganja, which is one of the oldest known synonyms for Marijuana, which most Bruce Lee fans admit Bruce Lee used on a number of occasions during his life. In a letter dated August 23rd of the same year, he also states: "...By the way the "G" in Bangkok is holy indeed. I understand Hong Kong is super lousy." (9). Hong Kong at the time had a very strict drug law. However, Thailand was a lot more lax in cracking down on the drug trade. In the same letter, we get to read for the first time Bruce talking about Robert Baker flying to Hong Kong while Bruce is filming his second movie, Fist of Fury, in which Robert would end up starring opposite Bruce as the Russian bad guy Petrov.

Once Bruce had moved to Hong Kong, his letters to Robert got less cryptic: "... Still am in the process of adapting to life here. By the way, what is the advice on the possibility of shipping some coke to me? Drop me a line on that." (10). When Bruce is saying Coke, he is referring to Cocaine. In one of the most important letters in the collection, sent to Robert in late 1972, Bruce goes into great detail about drugs: "(A) Regarding the goods — you can send them in a package addressed to Mr. Wu Ngan, c/o Golden Harvest Studio, 1412 Tung Ying Building 100 Nathan Rd. The goodies list can be (1) COKE (in large amount) (2) ACID (in fair amount) (3) HASH OR GRASS (the former can be more while the latter, even cleaned, has to be carefully packed. As to what you put the above with you know better — inside books? Clothings? —

(B) Also, when I come I would like to have more goodies ready for shipping including finding me a really classy Derringer — from shops, collection, or what not. Also, find me a cowboy holster for my 45 fast draw — all these when I come, but not for your sending me right away.

So send (A) request right away ... they might open for brief inspection or they might not — but play it safe. As for the total cost, let me know and I'll send you the money order by air mail right away. P.S. Do you have access to any PSILO-CYBIN? If so send a little together with info on how to take it. Read about it in a book." (11). Not only is the letter quite shocking, where Bruce openly asks Robert to send him various drugs in various

13

Bob,

Air-mail me some Coca-Cola — do it the way you and I sincerely feel — in other word, whatever. Be cool about the package, same procedure Wu Ngan — "quality! man" What n...

14

Bob,

Been resting and reading your book that you've sent. By now you should have received my money order though I feel that it might be a slight delay because of your friend's situation. I hope you will send me the "quality" stuff you said you will send ("it has never been from the street"). In the meantime I'm getting a "quality" spoon and a Quad-raveam scale. Do send it "AIR-MAIL" like yesterday (HA! HA!)

Take good care my friend
Bruce

---

amounts, but also states he wants a weapon. Was Bruce getting more paranoid and wanted another gun for protection? It even shows that Bruce was starting to try other drugs, including PSILOCYBIN, more infamously known as Magic Mushrooms. Bruce even makes sure that the drugs don't get delivered to his address, but to the address of Golden Harvest Movie Studios, in the name of his assistant/friend Wu Ngan.

The letters sent by Linda Lee, Bruce's wife, were just as shocking as the letters sent by Bruce, a letter dated October 2, 1972, states: "I just want to check with you about the second shipment. We thought you probably would have sent it already, but it has not arrived. Hope nothing has happened to it in the mail. Please confirm if you have sent it or not. In regards to the money, I'll send as soon as I can get to the bank to buy a money order." (12). And in another letter Bruce sent to Robert on December 11, 1972, he says; "Air-mail me some Coca-Cola — do it the way you and I sincerely feel — in other word, whatever. Be cool about the package. Same procedure, Wu Ngan — "quality! man" and in another letter written not long after: "Cooly" send some Coke — How's everything? Stoned as hell, but am working on the upcoming character. Some coke would help in the formation and what I want to create."

At this stage, the letters from Bruce seemed to be more about drugs, than his friendship with Robert, and in some of the letters, you could feel the desperation for more shipments to be sent over. In a letter dated early 1973, Bruce is clearly responding to Robert's previous letter stating that one of his friends had been arrested on drugs charges: "Deep regret for your friend being busted," Bruce carries on by saying: "RUSH the sparkle "quality" LOTS!" and on the opposite side of the page he says: "By now you should have received my money order, though I feel that it might be a slight delay because of your friend's situation. I hope you will send me the "quality" stuff you said you will send ("it has never been from the street"). In the meantime I'm getting a "quality" spoon and a quad- scale. Do send it "air-mail" like yesterday (ha! ha!)" It seems at this point that Bruce was more interested in getting his shipment than Robert getting into trouble, which is a shame, considering how close Robert and Bruce had become,

April 14, 1973

Dear Bob,

It's been quite a while since you've written. I assume you have received the money order for $500 and I am wondering if you have sent the C yet. Please let me know right away because if you did not receive the money order then I will have to tell the bank to put a tracer on it.

How are you all doing? We hope things are straightening out for you. Say thanks to Bev for taking the risk and sending the last shipment to Bruce. <u>Don't worry about Bruce using the C — he is not going overboard.</u>

---

it seemed Bruce trusted Robert more than most people around him at that time.

In another letter from Linda to Robert, dated March 29, 1973, Bruce is busy shooting Enter the Dragon, but still corresponding regarding Cocaine: "Received your four letters. Bruce is in the midst of shooting — working very hard. Well, forget about your making some money out of the last orders. I've bought a gram measurer and enclosed you will find the $500 for the amount of C you quote that Bruce can get. I'll measure it but the quality (that goes without saying) plus the quantity Bruce himself will have to judge. I hope you will send him the mostest along with the one oz of H. oil and/or whatever." H oil, refers to Hash oil, also known as honey oil or cannabis oil. Then two weeks later on April 16, Linda writes again: "Dear

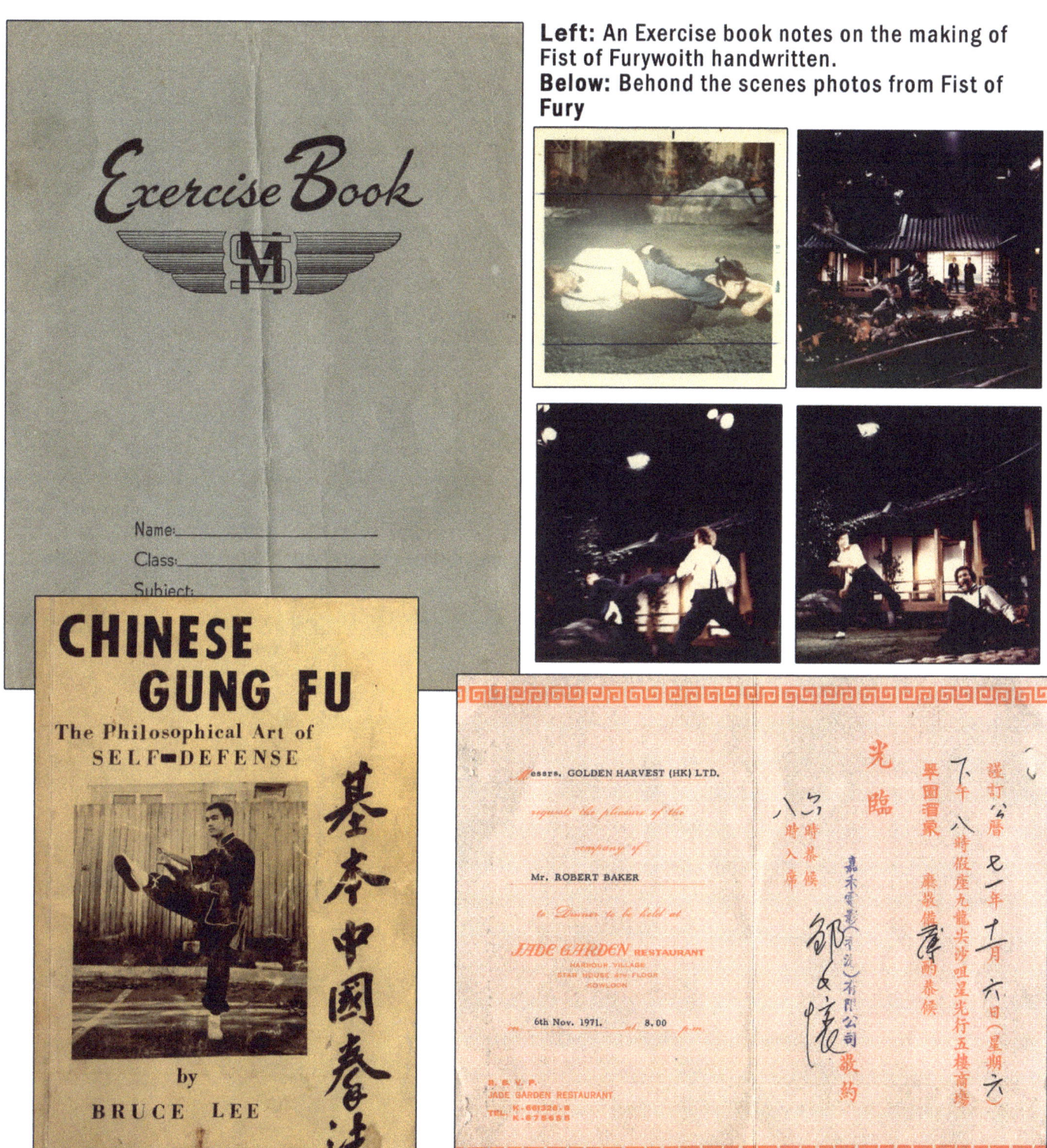

Left: An Exercise book notes on the making of Fist of Furywoith handwritten.
Below: Behond the scenes photos from Fist of Fury

Above Left: A 1st edition copy pf Bruce Lee's Chinese Gung Fu.
Above Right: A invetation to Robert Wall from Golden Harvest, for a dinner to be held in his honor.

Bob, It's been quite a while since you've written. I assume you have received the money order for $500 and I am wondering if you have sent the C yet. Please let me know right away because if you did not receive the money order, then I will have to talk to the bank to put a tracer on it. How are you all doing? We hope things are straightening out for you. Say thanks to Bev for taking the risk and sending the last shipment to Bruce. Don't worry about Bruce using the C — he is not going overboard. Write very soon and let us know about the $500 money order and/or when the C is coming." Why was Robert starting to ignore Bruce and Linda? Were things getting too dangerous to smuggle drugs from America to Hong Kong? And was Robert starting to worry about how many drugs Bruce was using?

Less than a month after Robert received Linda's last letter on May 10, 1973, Bruce Lee collapsed and suffered seizures and headaches. Two months later after suffering more headaches, Bruce was dead. Unfortunately for a lot of Bruce Lee fans, these letters indicate that Bruce was not only taking various drugs, but more seriously, that he was dealing and trafficking in them. It is safe to say, that during the 1960s and 70s, most notable celebrities partook in recreational drugs, so it's not surprising Bruce also did. What is surprising was how drugs seemed to become a major part of Bruce Lee's everyday life, and that it got worse nearer to his passing, which certainly puts more emphasis on the mysterious circumstances of his death.

FURY OF THE DRAGON

Review (1976) By Rick baker

The movie was intended to pay homage to the late Bruce Lee and his undeniable martial arts skills. Released in 1976, nine years after the end of the television series "THE GREEN HORNET," the film was created by stitching together four random episodes of the show and releasing them theatrically as a tribute to Bruce Lee, who had passed away three years earlier. Despite the film's efforts to showcase Bruce Lee, the editing and lack of continuity make it difficult to fully appreciate his performances. The film jumps from one episode to the next, leaving the audience confused and disoriented. Additionally, the episodes chosen for the film were not selected for their quality or relevance to the overall story, leading to a disjointed and jarring viewing experience. However, for die-hard fans of Bruce Lee, FURY OF THE DRAGON is a must-see film. It serves as a showcase of his martial arts skills and screen presence, and the film opens with a screen test of Lee's from 1965, which earned him the role of Kato in the television series. The film is a hodge-podge of episodes from the television series, but despite its lack of coherence and continuity, it still serves as a fitting tribute to the late Bruce Lee.

But to be completely honest "FURY OF THE DRAGON" is a poorly executed film that is only recommended for die-hard fans of Bruce Lee. The film's lack of coherence and continuity may be a disappointment, but it still serves as a fitting tribute to the late martial arts legend and his undeniable screen presence.

BRUCE IS AGAIN
◎埋もれていた〈アメリカ主演作品〉
◎ついに発見!「若き日のブルース・リー」
◎甦えった鉄拳が挑む殺人科学兵器!
◎全篇をつらぬくスーパー・メカニック
アメリカ・LLBJMエンタープライズ作品
FURY OF THE DRAGON
ブルース・リー
電光石火

EV
DRAGON
FURY OF THE DRAGON
BRUCE LEE IN
Fury OF THE DRAGON
VHS
BRUCE LEE AND VAN WILLIAMS
EXECUTIVE PRODUCER LAURENCE JOACHIM
DIRECTED BY WILLIAM BEAUDINE

NUR MIT DEM ECHTEN, WAHREN BRUCE LEE
Sensationelle Karate-Kämpfe mit dem Idol von Millionen
UNCUT!
BRUCE LEE
DER GELBE TAIFUN

BRUCE LEE IS KATO
FURY OF THE DRAGON
Found on CineMaterial.com

DOUBLE FEATURE
BRUCE LEE IS KATO
THE GREEN HORNET
BRUCE LEE IS KATO
FURY OF THE DRAGON
M
DVD

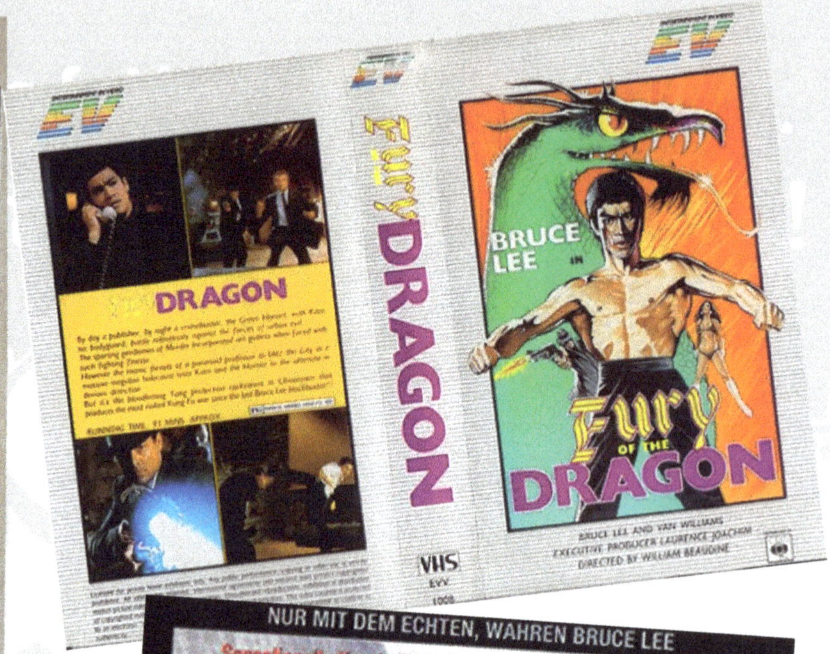

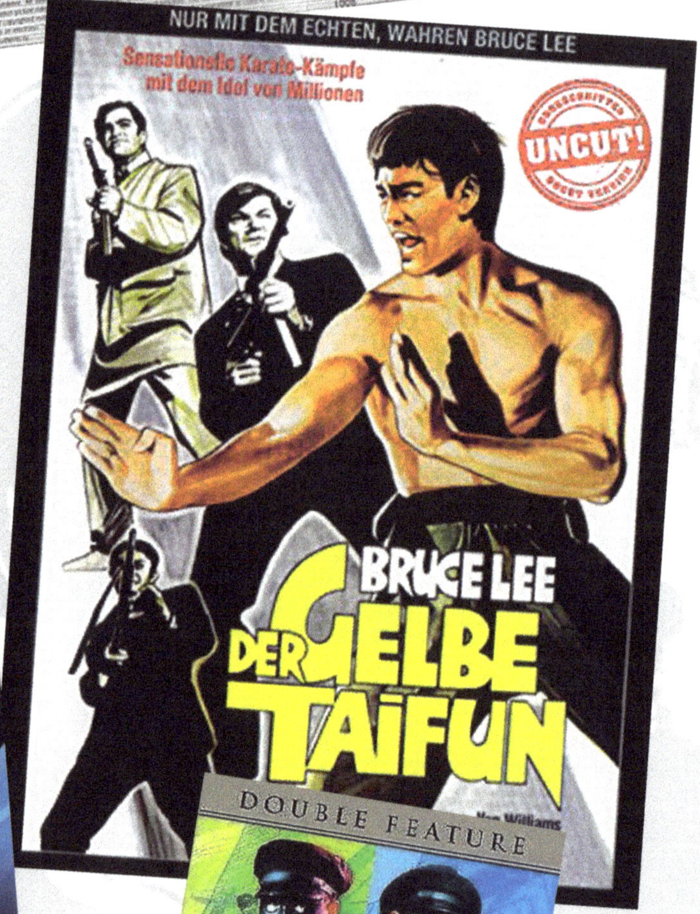

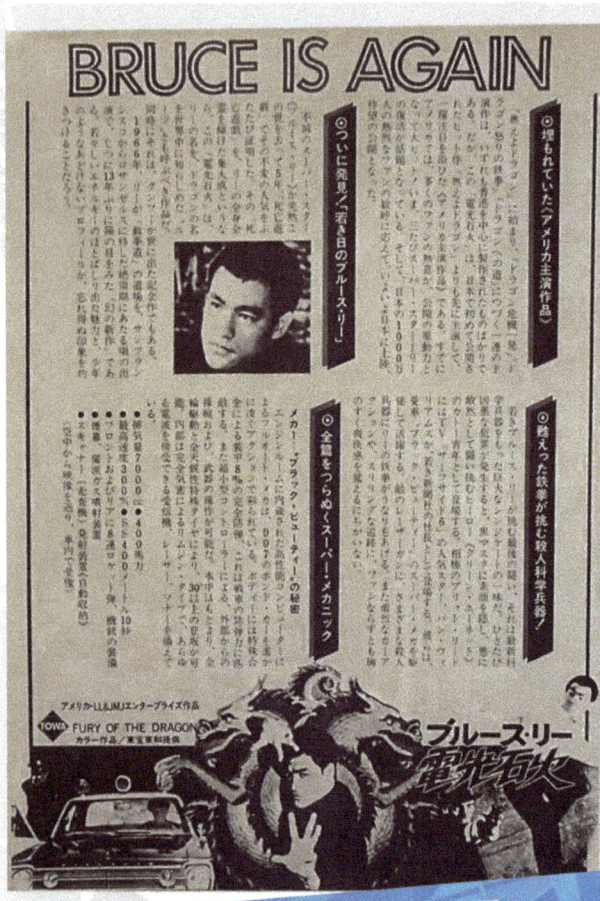

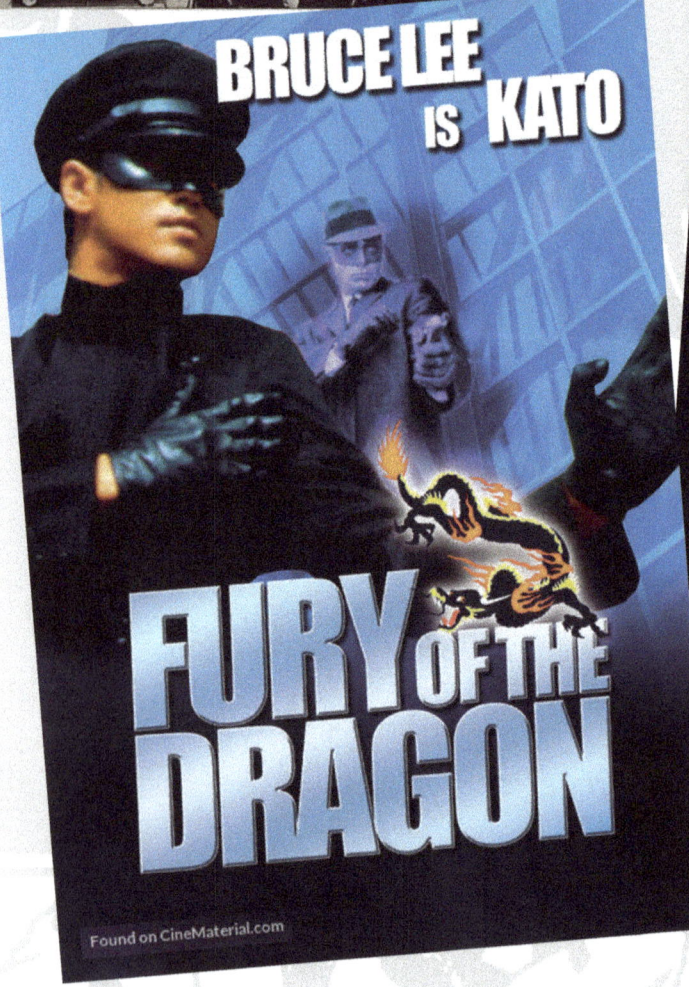

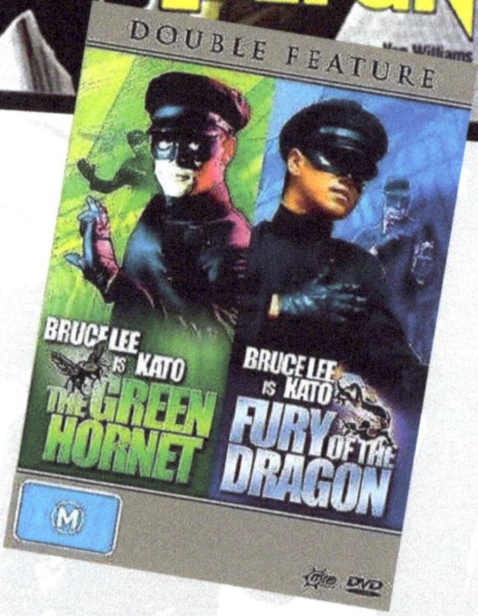

The Green Hornet

Review By Rick Baker

TV movie, that combines elements of crime-fighting, science fiction, and comedy. The film follows the story of Britt Reid, a newspaper editor and TV station head who dons a mask and becomes the Green Hornet, a crime-fighting vigilante who uses hi-tech gadgets and a powerful car, Black Beauty, to fight crime. The film begins with Reid investigating a series of murders of the heads of the city's crime rackets, which leads him to a connection with the Explorers Club. However, the situation quickly becomes complicated when a UFO crashes outside the city and the supposed aliens take Reid's secretary hostage and demand that he make a television broadcast to calm the populace.
It turn out, the aliens are a scheme masterminded by a disgraced nuclear scientist Dr Eric Mabouse, and the UFO crash is a cover to hijack a Air force transport of an H-bomb. Meanwhile, Reid also gets caught in the middle of a tong war in Chinatown.

The Green Hornet (1974) is a unique blend of genres, and while it may not have the most cohesive plot, it manages to be an entertaining and enjoyable film. The acting is solid, particularly from Bruce Lee as Kato, and the film's special effects are impressive for the time. The film also features a good balance of action and comedy, with some tongue-in-cheek humor and campy moments throughout the movie.
Overall, The Green Hornet (1974) may not be a classic, but it is an entertaining and fun film that is definitely worth checking out for fans of the genre. If you are looking for a blend of crime fighting, science fiction and comedy in a single movie, this is definitely a film that is worth a watch.

Thomas Gross
The German Connection

"I would like to give a big thank you to Thomas Gross for taking the time to allow us to present his fabulous and rare "Green Hornet" memorabilia. There are some excellent examples being showcased that I am sure will make great viewing for any collector of Bruce Lee items or collectors of The Green Hornet TV show."

Sensationelle Karate-Kämpfe mit dem Idol von Millionen
BRUCE LEE
DER GELBE TAIFUN
FSK
Constantin-Film

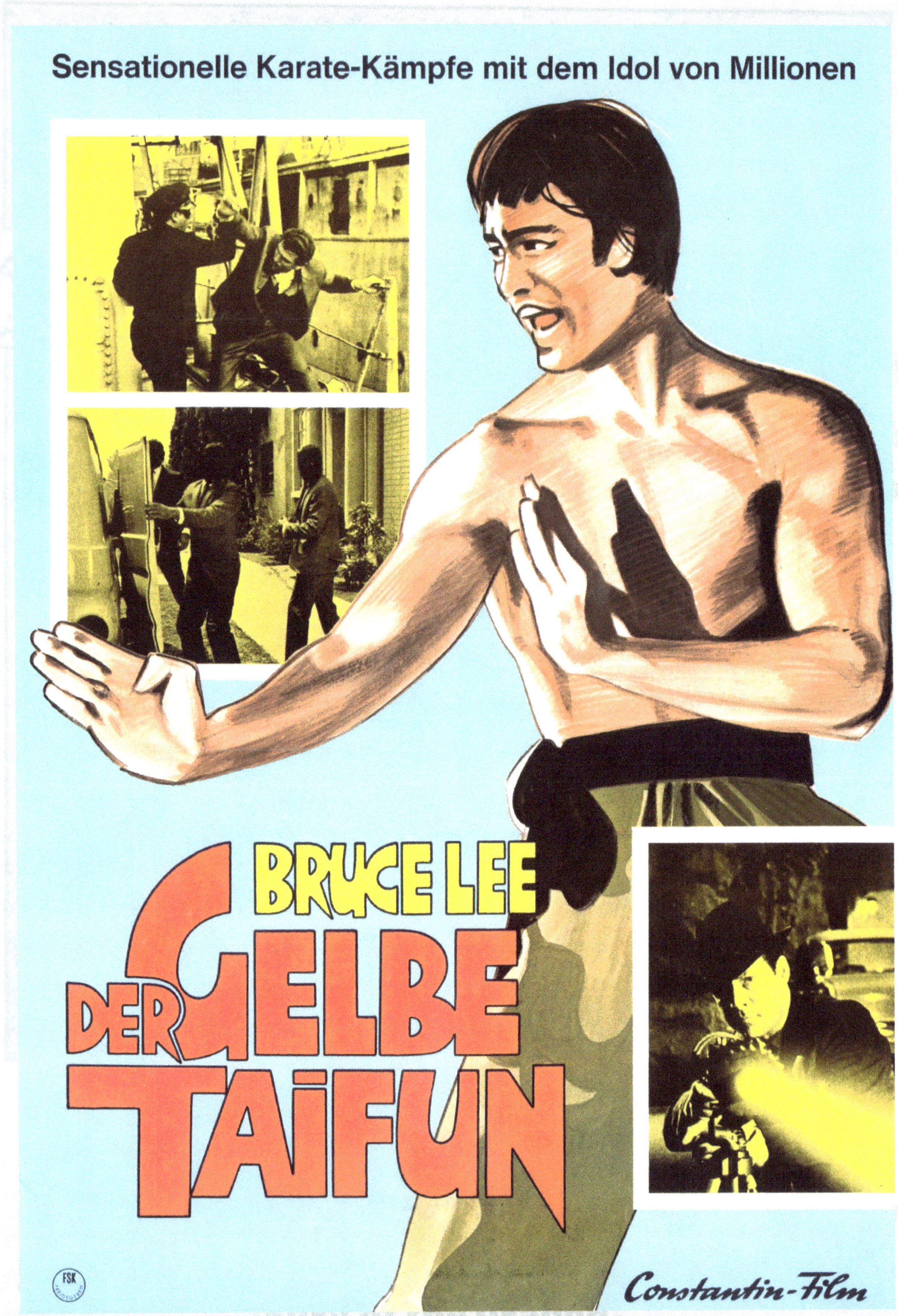

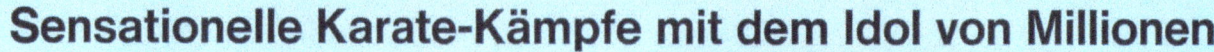

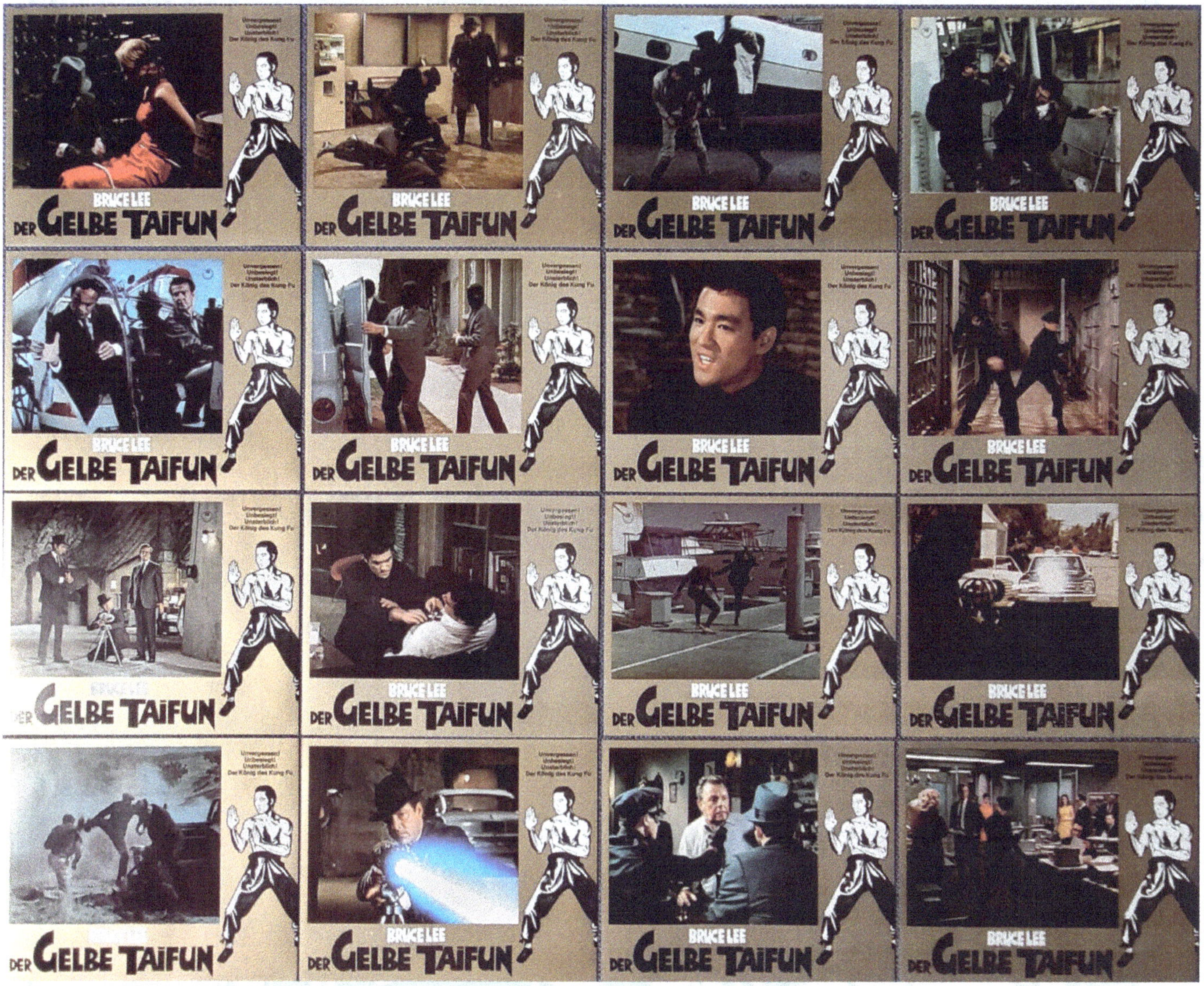
Unvergessen! Unbesiegt! Unsterblich! Der König des Kung Fu
BRUCE LEE
DER GELBE TAIFUN

Bruce Lee
DAS GEHEIMNIS DER GRÜNEN HORNISSE

Bruce Lee
DAS GEHEIMNIS DER GRÜNEN HORNISSE

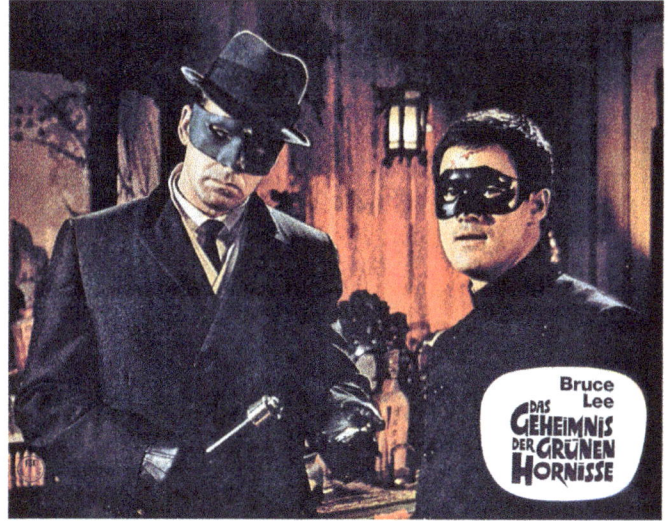

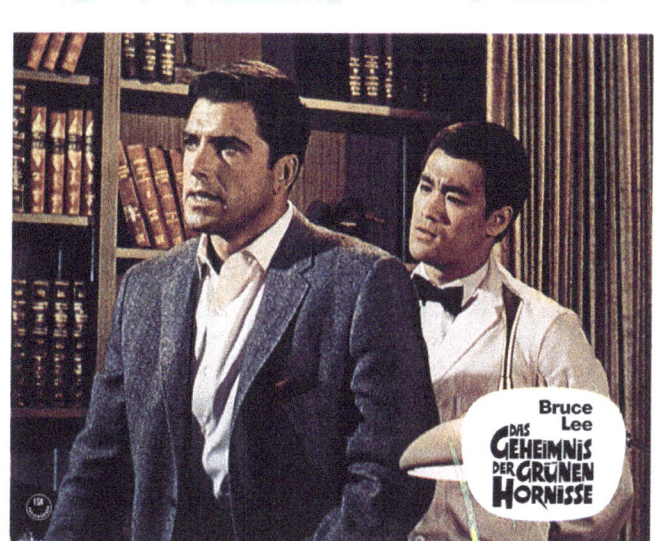

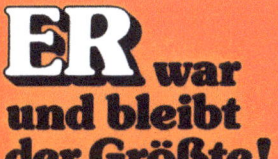

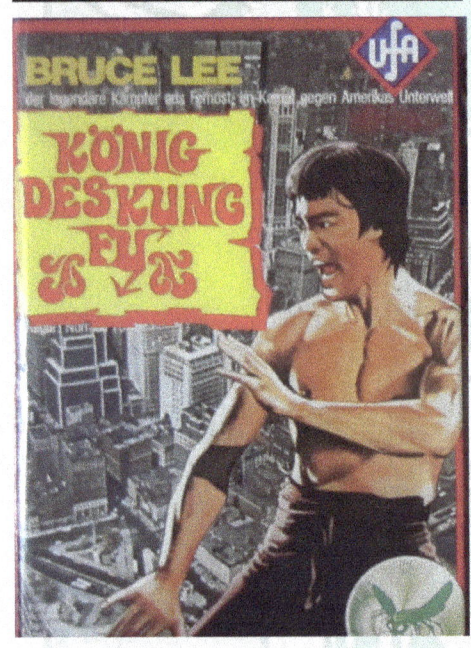

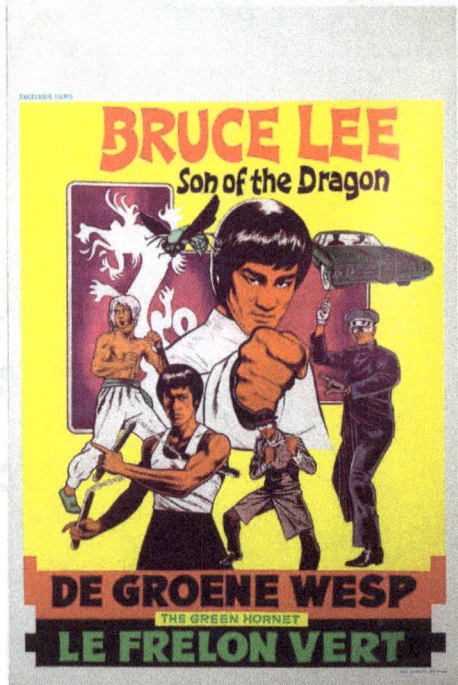

IL 20 LUGLIO 1973 SI SPEGNEVA A HONG KONG
BRUCE LEE
Qualche giorno più tardi accompagnato dal suo inseparabile amico STEVE McQUEEN veniva sotterrato a Seattle in U.S.A. STEVE McQUEEN inchinandosi davanti alla sua bara pronunciò queste parole

« Bruce la morte non ti ucciderà! »

sono passati più di 2 anni e possiamo confermare che le parole di STEVE McQUEEN SI SONO AVVERATE

PER I GIOVANI DI TUTTO IL MONDO É DIVENTATO UN PERSONAGGIO DA LEGGENDA

La P.A.B. FILM é lieta di presentare
L'UNICO SUO FILM ANCORA INEDITO IN ITALIA

LA FURIA DEL DRAGO

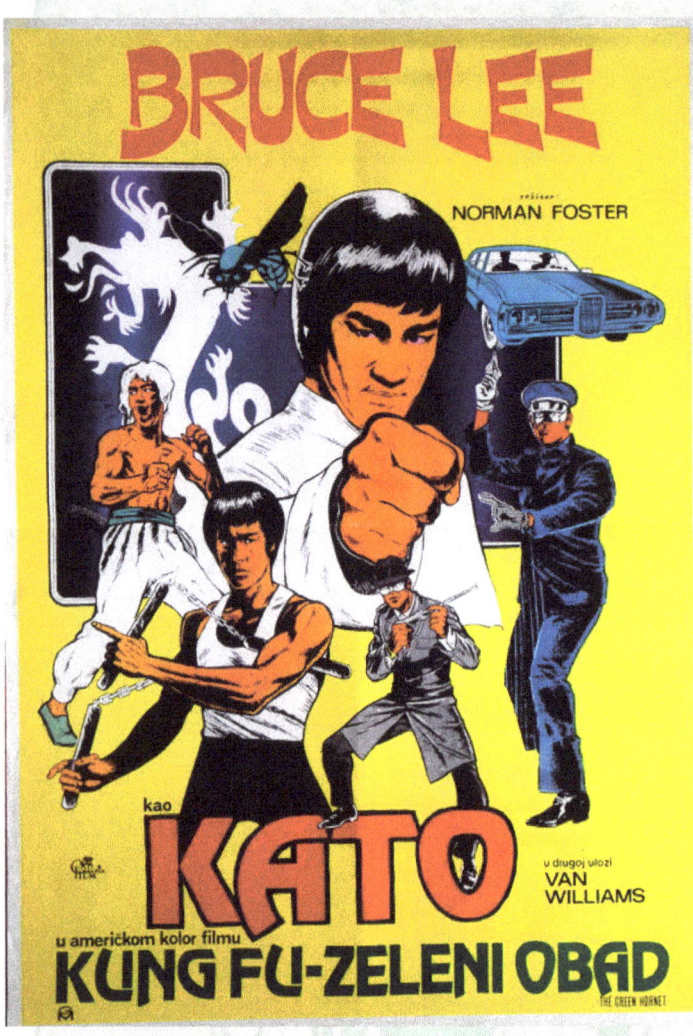

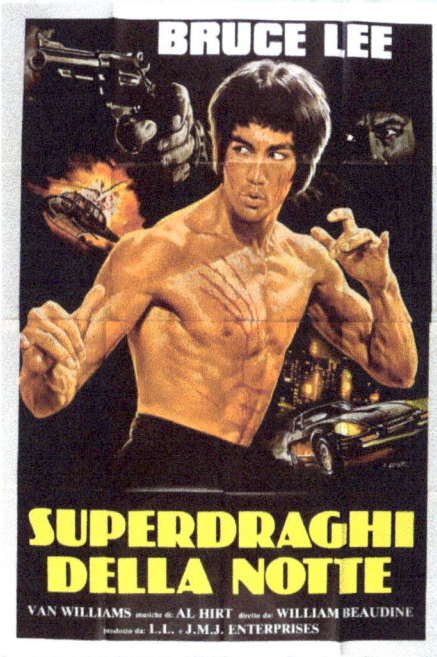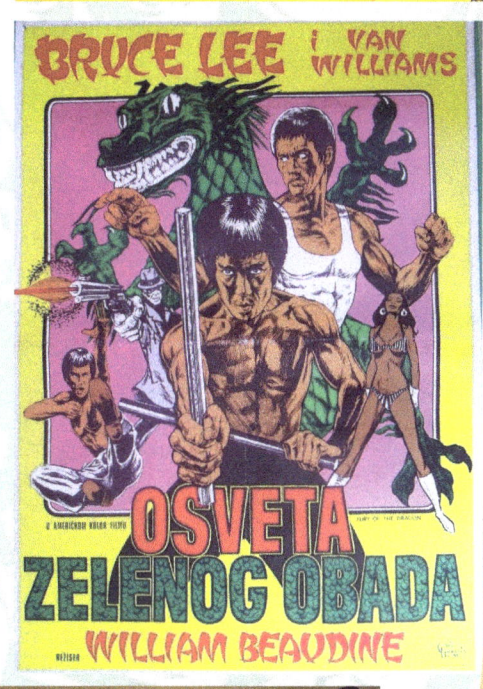

BRUCE LEE
SUPERDRAGHI DELLA NOTTE

VAN WILLIAMS musiche di: AL HIRT
diretto da: WILLIAM BEAUDINE
prodotto da: L.L. e J.M.J. ENTERPRISES

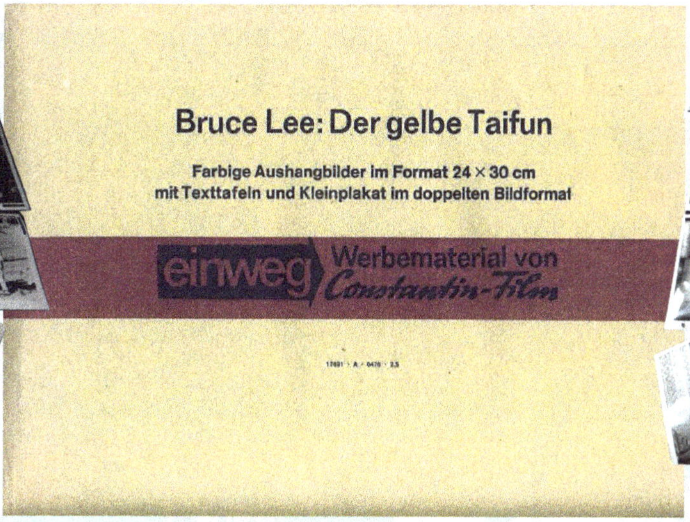
Bruce Lee: Der gelbe Taifun
Farbige Aushangbilder im Format 24 × 30 cm
mit Texttafeln und Kleinplakat im doppelten Bildformat
einweg
Werbematerial von
Constantin-Film

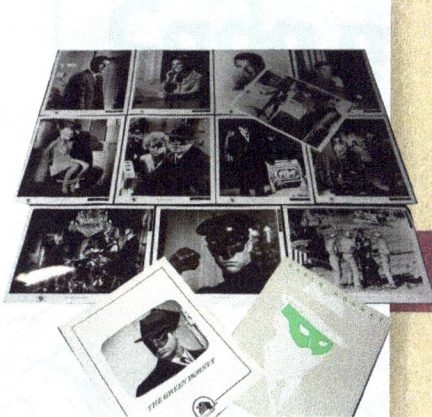

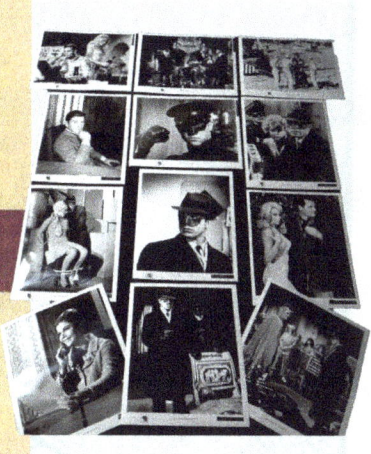

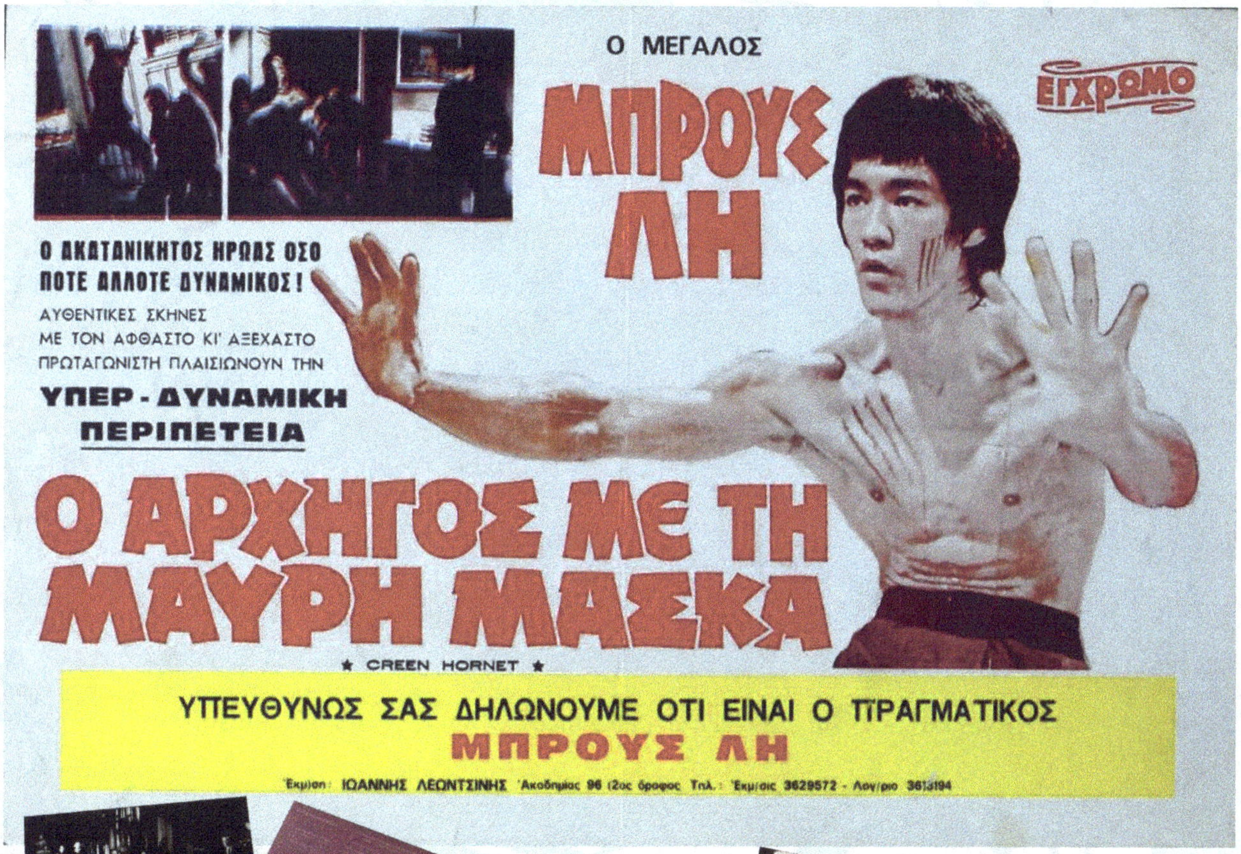
Ο ΜΕΓΑΛΟΣ
ΜΠΡΟΥΣ ΛΗ
ΕΓΧΡΩΜΟ
Ο ΑΚΑΤΑΝΙΚΗΤΟΣ ΗΡΩΑΣ ΟΣΟ ΠΟΤΕ ΑΛΛΟΤΕ ΔΥΝΑΜΙΚΟΣ!
ΑΥΘΕΝΤΙΚΕΣ ΣΚΗΝΕΣ ΜΕ ΤΟΝ ΑΦΘΑΣΤΟ ΚΙ' ΑΞΕΧΑΣΤΟ ΠΡΩΤΑΓΩΝΙΣΤΗ ΠΛΑΙΣΙΩΝΟΥΝ ΤΗΝ
ΥΠΕΡ-ΔΥΝΑΜΙΚΗ ΠΕΡΙΠΕΤΕΙΑ
Ο ΑΡΧΗΓΟΣ ΜΕ ΤΗ ΜΑΥΡΗ ΜΑΣΚΑ
★ CREEN HORNET ★
ΥΠΕΥΘΥΝΩΣ ΣΑΣ ΔΗΛΩΝΟΥΜΕ ΟΤΙ ΕΙΝΑΙ Ο ΠΡΑΓΜΑΤΙΚΟΣ
ΜΠΡΟΥΣ ΛΗ
Έκμ/ση: ΙΩΑΝΝΗΣ ΛΕΟΝΤΣΙΝΗΣ Ακοδημίας 96 (2ος όροφος Τηλ.: Έκμ/σις 3629572 - Λογ/ριο 3613194

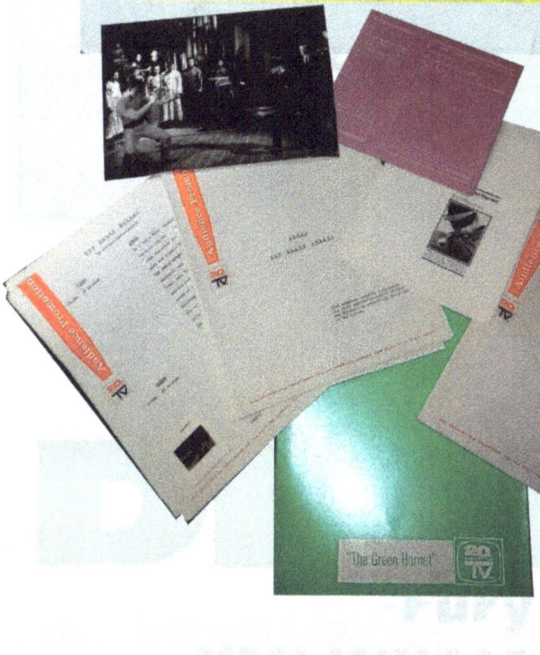
"The Green Hornet"

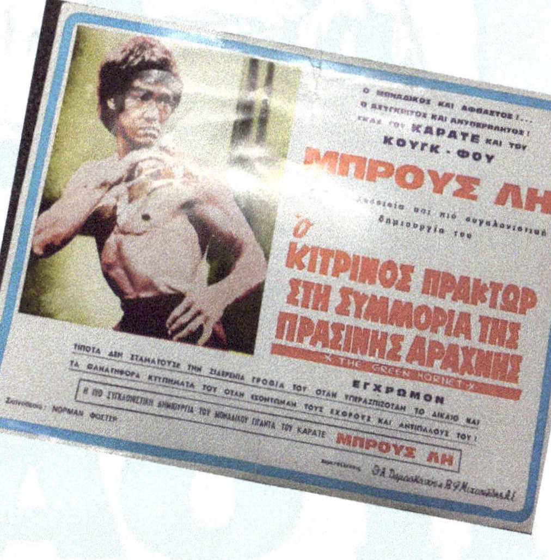
ΚΑΡΑΤΕ
ΚΟΥΓΚ - ΦΟΥ
ΜΠΡΟΥΣ ΛΗ
ΚΙΤΡΙΝΟΣ ΠΡΑΚΤΩΡ ΣΤΗ ΣΥΜΜΟΡΙΑ ΤΗΣ ΠΡΑΣΙΝΗΣ ΑΡΑΧΝΗΣ
ΕΓΧΡΩΜΟΝ
ΜΠΡΟΥΣ ΛΗ

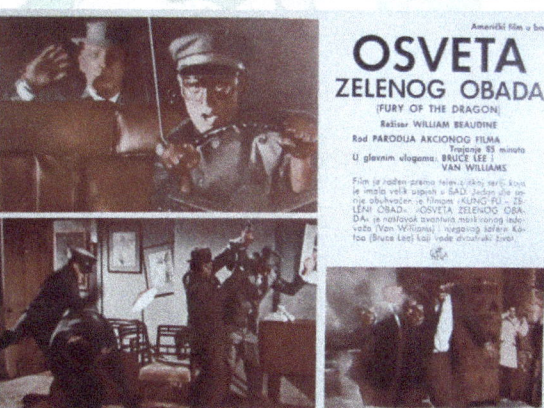

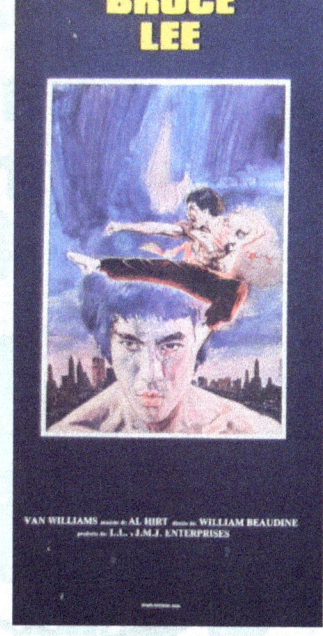

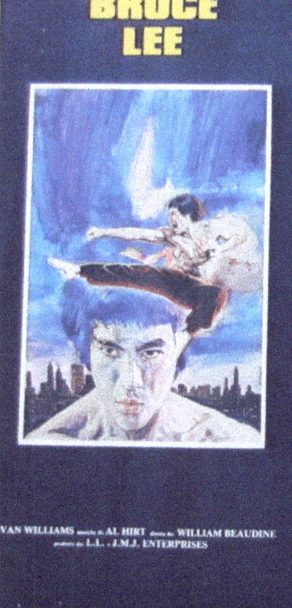

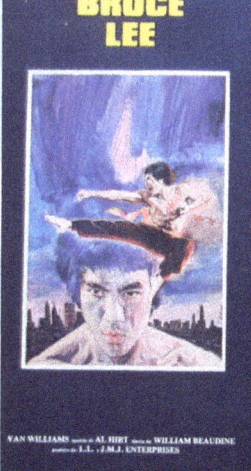

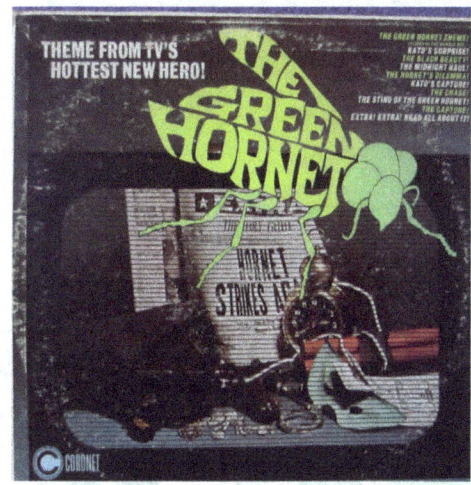

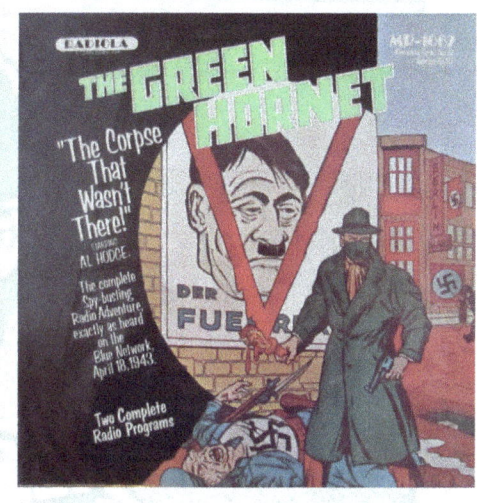
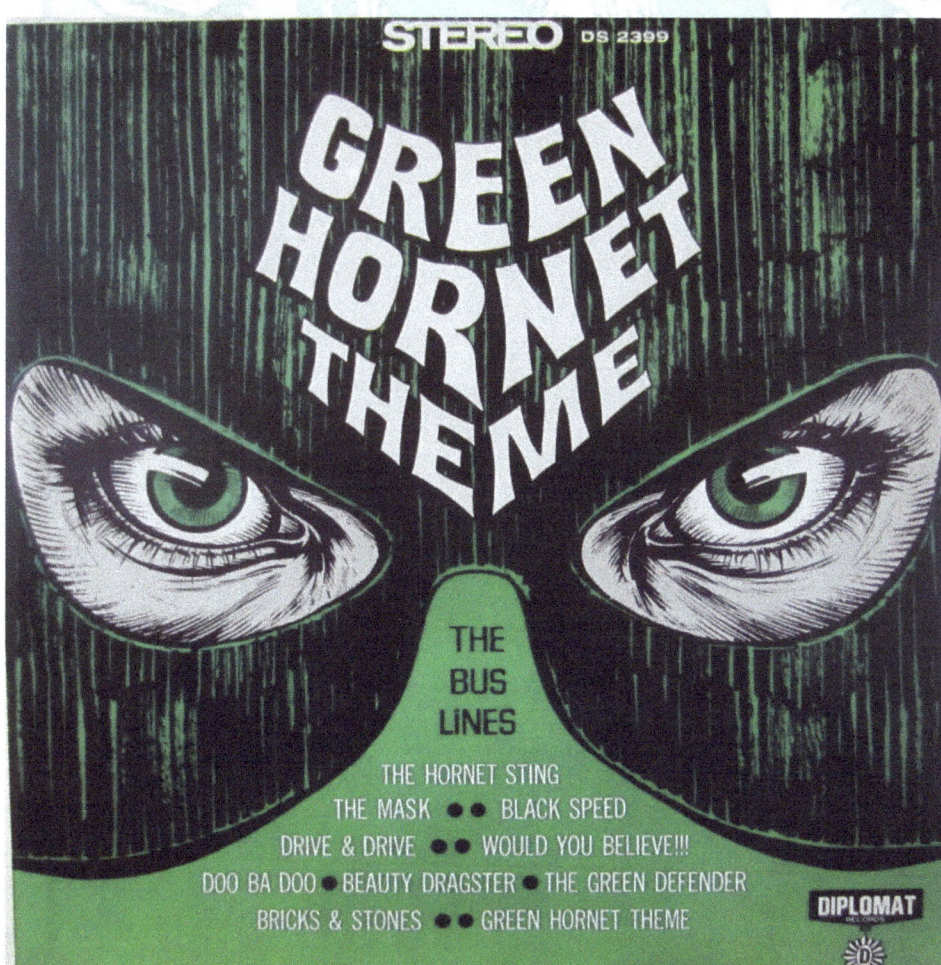

BRUCE LEE ES KATO EL AVISPÓN VERDE

FRASES

- BRUCE LEE es KATO (El Avispón Verde)

Puños asesinos y patadas vengadoras es el ataque de Kato.

- El Rey del Kung Fu siempre es el vencedor, el porqué? Véalo.

- Bruce Lee saca el Kung Fu de la obscuridad en que la gente lo quería mantener.

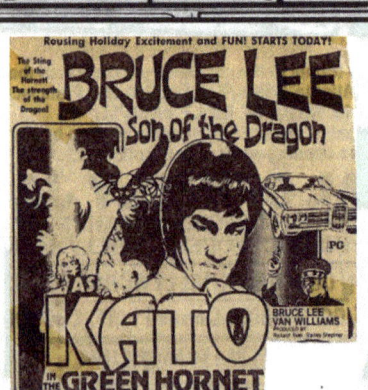

film-echo FILMWOCH

vereinigt mit *filmblätter*

1 Y 28
25. Juli
Einzelpreis 2,5

Termine zum Vormerken:

25.7.
Bruce Lee, der legendäre Kämpfer aus Fernost, in einem harten Gangster-Film
BRUCE LEE: DAS GEHEIMNIS DER GRÜNEN HORNISSE
Bruce Lee, Van Williams, Walter Brooks u. v. a.
Regie: Norman Foster · Produktion: Trans-National, New York

8.8.
Groß, blond und leicht durch den Wind: PIERRE RICHARD in seinen neuesten Abenteuern
ALFRED, DIE KNALLERBSE
Pierre Richard, Anny Duperey, Pierre Mondy u. v. a.
Regie: Pierre Richard · Produktion: Gaumont/La Guéville/Madeleine, Paris

22.8.
Ein Militär-Lustspiel voller toller Überraschungen
HERR OBERST HABEN EINE MACKE!
Aldo Maccione, Jacques Dufilho, Franco Dilogne, Marius Marenco, Silvio Spaccesi u. v. a.
Regie: Mino Guerrini · Produktion: Coralta, Rom/Fox Europa, Paris

22.8.
Der Höhepunkt einer einzigartigen Erfolgsserie – die intimsten Geheimnisse junger Mädchen
SCHULMÄDCHEN-REPORT 9. TEIL
Reifeprüfung vor dem Abitur
Regie: Walter Boos · Produktion: Rapid-Film, München

29.8.
Die fesselnde Geschichte eines Mädchens, das sein Glück macht
DAS MÄDCHEN KEETJE TIPPEL
mit den Stars der »Türkischen Früchte« Monique van de Ven, Rutger Hauer u. v. a.
Regie: Paul Verhoeven · Produktion: Rob Houwer-Film

Bitte sichern Sie sich IHRE Kopien!

Constantin-Film

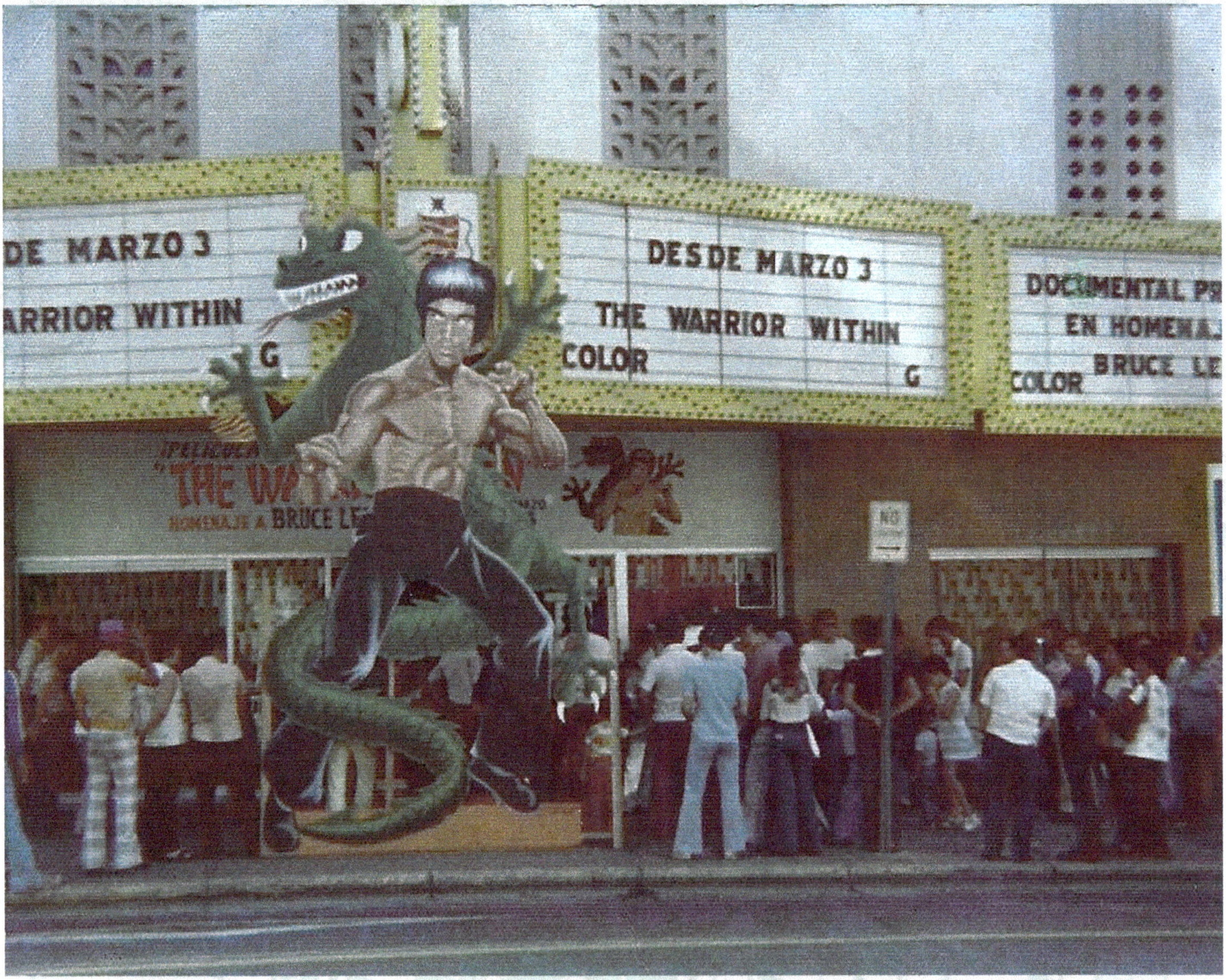
DE MARZO 3
ARRIOR WITHIN
G
DESDE MARZO 3
THE WARRIOR WITHIN
COLOR
G
DOCUMENTAL PR
EN HOMENAJ
BRUCE LE
COLOR
HOMENAJE A BRUCE LE

FIRST SHOWING
BRUCE LEE
KATO
THE GREEN HORNET
HE STINGS LIKE A HORNET...HAS THE STRENGTH OF A DRAGON!

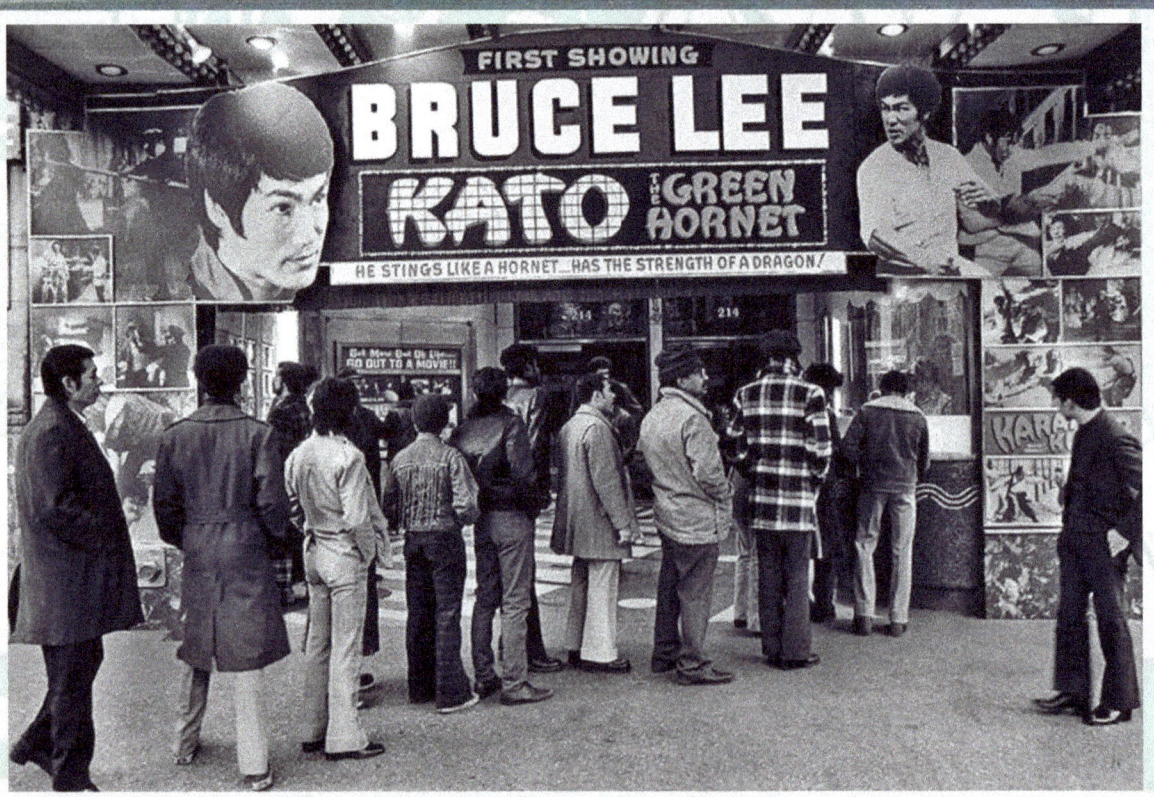

THE GREEN HORNET
OVERVIEW & EPISODES
By Rick Baker

When it comes to the cult classic television shows, one series that immediately comes to mind is "The Green Hornet." This crime-fighting show, which originally aired in the 1960s, starred Van Williams as the wealthy playboy-turned-vigilante, Britt Reid, and Bruce Lee as his skilled martial artist sidekick, Kato. Although it was only on the air for one season, the series has left a lasting impact on popular culture and continues to be beloved by fans to this day.

Bruce Lee as the character Kato is considered a cult classic for a few reasons. Firstly, the show features Bruce Lee in his first major acting role, which helped to introduce him to a wider audience and cement his status as a martial arts icon. Secondly, the show was one of the first American television shows to feature an Asian American lead character, which was ground-breaking for its time. Thirdly, the series is also notable for its campy tone and over-the-top action, which has since become iconic among fans of the genre.

One aspect of the show that has particularly stood the test of time is the theme music. Years after the show went off the air; the theme from "The Horn Meets the Hornet" was featured in the highly-acclaimed film, Kill Bill Vol. 1, directed by Quentin Tarantino. In this movie, Tarantino paid homage to Kato by having a group of sword-fighting antagonists, known as "The Crazy 88", wear masks reminiscent of Kato's during an intense battle scene.

This inclusion in Kill Bill Vol. 1 is a testament to the enduring legacy of "The Green Hornet." The series, which was known for its blend of action and drama as well as its socially conscious storylines, continues to resonate with audiences decades later. And of course, Bruce Lee's portrayal of Kato as a skilled and resourceful ally, helped to introduce

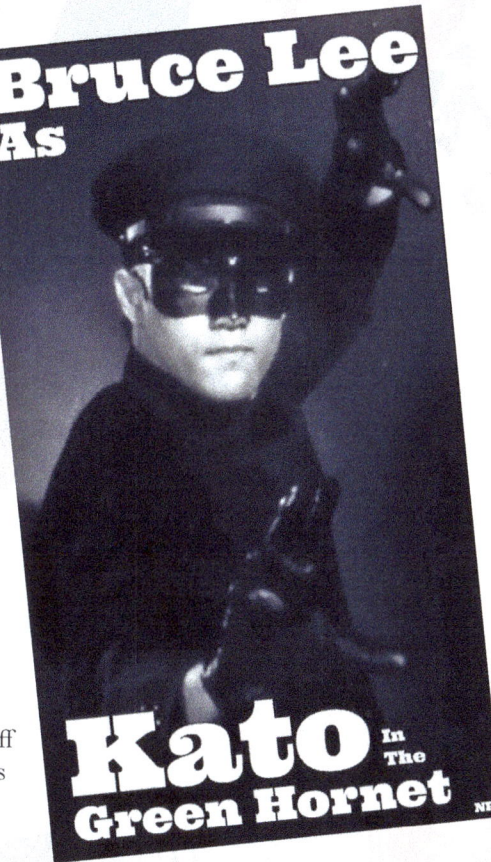

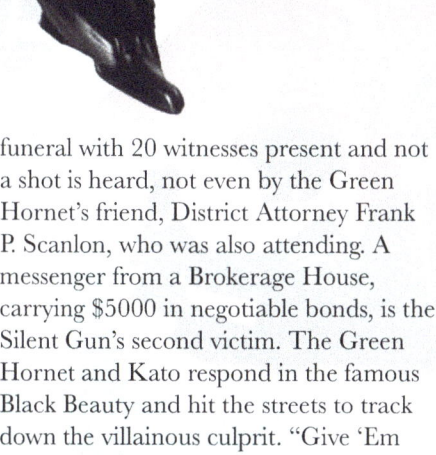

martial arts to the American audiences, making the character an iconic figure in popular culture. Unlike Batman, The Green Hornet was played straight rather than tongue-in-cheek. That may well have been the series downfall
TV Episodes. Title and Plot.
"The Silent Gun" In this premiere episode, Dave Bannister is shot at a funeral with 20 witnesses present and not a shot is heard, not even by the Green Hornet's friend, District Attorney Frank P. Scanlon, who was also attending. A messenger from a Brokerage House, carrying $5000 in negotiable bonds, is the Silent Gun's second victim. The Green Hornet and Kato respond in the famous Black Beauty and hit the streets to track down the villainous culprit. "Give 'Em

Enough Rope" Joe Sweek, waiting to meet Daily Sentinel reporter Mike Axford to sell him photos proving an insurance claim to be fraudulent, is manipulated into a nearby warehouse and murdered by a man in black swinging from a rope. The Green Hornet plans a surprise visit to the claimant, Alex Colony, to propose a partnership with him in his "accident" racket.

"Programmed for Death" After reporter Pat Allen is killed in the Daily Sentinel's eighth-floor city room by a leopard, Britt Reid finds a transmitter in a cigarette box. Later, D.A. Scanlon informs Britt of the discovery of a perfect diamond on Allen's desk. Digging around, Reid suspects that the gemmologist had been working on producing synthetic diamonds, and the Green Hornet takes an interest in him. Although the third episode aired by ABC, this is generally believed to be the series' original pilot, in part due to the fact that stars Van Williams and Bruce Lee wear angularly stylized masks rather than those moulded to their faces seen in other episodes.[15] This episode was also released as a Sawyers' View Master stereoscopic set.

"Crime Wave" A scientist predicts crimes with a computer that implicates the Green Hornet.

"The Frog Is a Deadly Weapon" Private investigator Nat Pyle informs Britt that he has proof, for a fee, that presumed-dead racketeer Glen Connors is still alive. Shortly later, Nat is found floating dead in the harbour from a possible boating accident. Reid thinks otherwise, and has a special interest in proving Pyle was murdered because it was Connors who had framed Reid's father, leading to the father's imprisonment and death.

"Eat, Drink, and Be Dead" An illegal bootleg liquor ring devised by Henry Dirk forces a stronghold on bars in the town to buy from them. As reporter Mike Axford tries to follow a lead to the racketeers, he becomes kidnapped. To get in and save Axford, the Green Hornet approaches Dirk for a cut of his action. The bootlegger and his helicopter, from which he drops bombs on his non-conformists, is a challenge to the Black Beauty.

"Beautiful Dreamer: Part 1" Seems that wealthy and prominent members of the community have been executing

crimes and then forgetting that they ever happened - including Miss Case, who's hypnotised into nearly killing Britt. Eventually the District Attorney and the Green Hornet find that Peter Eden, owner of the very high class spa called the Vale of Eden, has been implanting "suggestions" into his clients's subconscious minds via his treatments. "Beautiful Dreamer: Part 2" Part two picks up with a Green Hornet visit and proposition for Peter Eden, owner of the Vale of Eden. After Peter uses Vanessa Vane in an almost successful attempt to double-cross the Hornet, the Hornet re-visits Eden and uses his own dream machine on Peter to foil the last crime for the evening and get him to confess everything to the police.

"The Ray Is for Killing" A charity art auction of fine paintings at Britt Reid's home is interrupted on live television by three masked, gun-toting criminals. The police, nearby, manage to wound one of the thieves, but before they can arrest the other two, a laser ray is unleashed on their squad car with devastating results. The Green Hornet and Kato find themselves in quite a confrontation against this portable killing machine - especially after Miss Case, whom the Hornet sent to track them with a secret device, becomes their hostage.

"The Preying Mantis" Organized crime's "Protection" Boss Duke Slate decides it's time to acquire "the city's Chinatown district" and uses Low Sing's tong to handle his influence. Low Sing, a martial arts professional, instructs his craft to his gang using the actions of a caged Praying Mantis, analogizing its intricate moves to proper Kung-Fu application. After a kidnapping which Low Sing engineers, a challenge between Low Sing and Kato is inevitable.

Keye Luke, the man who previously played Kato in the 1940s film serials and would later appear in Kung Fu as Caine's master in some flashback segments of the show, has an un-predicted role as Mr Chang. "The Hunters and the Hunted" Big-game hunters are using mobsters as quarry—but their next target may be their most dangerous game yet, the Green Hornet. "Deadline for Death" After a rash of wealthy homes are burglarized shortly after reporter Mike Axford writes a feature

"Freeway to Death" Britt Reid orders Mike Axford to team up with the Green Hornet to uncover the ringleader in an insurance scam. Mike reluctantly agrees, but later tries to expose the ringleader alone, leaving it up to the Green Hornet and Kato to save him before it is too late. Guest starring Jeffrey Hunter.

"May the Best Man Lose" At election time, District Attorney Scanlon is running for another term, but someone wants to remove him from the ballot - his challenger's brother, whom the challenger doesn't realise is willing to commit high crime as well as murder to help him win. "The Hornet and the Firefly" An arsonist wreaks havoc setting fire to buildings at the stroke of midnight. The Green Hornet and the District Attorney work behind the scenes to aid the Commissioner to put a stop to this hot situation. The Commissioner refuses to enlist the aid of a retired top arson investigator because his work had previously cost him an eye, but reporter Mike Axford suggests to Britt Reid that the Daily Sentinel can put him to work. Mike is in for a very big surprise. **"Seek, Stalk and Destroy"** A tank crew who served together in Korea steals a tank to free their former captain from prison before he is executed for the murder of their ex-commanding officer. It falls to the Green Hornet and Kato both to stop them before they can accomplish their goal, and to uncover the real killer.

"Corpse of the Year: Part 1" A carbon copy of the Green Hornet's Black Beauty attacks a Daily Sentinel delivery truck and terminates its driver right in front of Britt Reid. Then the Daily Sentinel offices have an explosive visit from a Green Hornet impostor, leading the real Green Hornet on a cat and mouse chase of his shadow car disrupting Daily Sentinel deliveries. Celia Kaye guest stars as Melissa Neal.

"Corpse of the Year: Part 2" After another death—of Simon Neal, publisher/owner of the Daily Express, at the hands of the phony Green Hornet, part 2 begins with Britt Reid bringing one of the Daily Express's previous employees, Dan Scully, into the Daily Sentinel's staff to help investigate Simon's termination. After finding out from Sabrina Bradley, Managing Editor of the Daily Express, that Simon had had a copy of the Black

Beauty produced for the Press Club's Masquerade Ball, the real Green Hornet sets a trap with her help.
"Ace in the Hole" When Mike Axford unexpectedly shows up at a meeting of mobsters Phil Trager, Steve Gant and the Green Hornet, he gets shot. The Hornet fools the other two into believing Mike has been killed and tries to manipulate them into taking each other out. The plan may fail and cost Axford, the Green Hornet, and Kato all their respective lives when the reporter reveals that he is still very much alive. Starring, Richard Anderson, and Richard X Slattery.

"**Bad Bet on a 459-Silent**" Britt Reid must figure out how to get medical attention for a wound he received as the Green Hornet, as well as how to stop two cops who are using silent alarm calls for their own profit.

"**Trouble for Prince Charming**" After the Green Hornet prevents the assassination of Prince Rafil, his blonde American fiancée, Janet Prescott, is kidnapped, and the prince is ordered to abdicate in order to save her.

"**Alias The Scarf**" When a wax museum's figure of The Scarf, an infamous strangler from 20 years ago, is replaced in the centre display spot by effigies of the Green Hornet and Kato, the waxen form of the Scarf seemingly comes to life and starts attacking people. Using the museum researcher's, manuscript about the Scarf, the Green Hornet and Kato attempt to snare the killer before he claims any more victims. Horror film star John Carradine plays the researcher.
"**Hornet Save Thyself**" As a surprise birthday party begins for Britt, a handgun given as a present to Britt seemingly discharges itself, fatally shooting ex-employee Eddie Rech. In a reverse of his usual situation, Britt Reid hides from the police by becoming the Green Hornet.
"Invasion from Outer Space: Part 1" The arrival of visitors from outer space seemingly coincides with an Air Force convoy transporting top secret electronic equipment and an H-Bomb missile warhead. Having Britt's secretary, Lenore "Casey" Case, taken hostage makes the situation very touchy. Brett King guest stars in this episode, his last screen role, as Major Jackson

"**Invasion from Outer Space: Part 2**" Part 2 begins with the Green Hornet using his tracking signal to close in on the visitors from outer space and their mystery. This is the last episode of the series. Batman and Robin on The Green Hornet In December 9, 1966 The Green Hornet episode "The Secret of the Sally Bell"[22] the Batmobile is seen on a television receiver, turning around inside the Batcave. In the February 3, 1967, Green Hornet episode "Ace in the Hole", which was transmitted in between the September 1966 and March 1967 Batman appearances (mentioned above), an unidentified episode of Batman is seen playing on a television set, showing Batman and Robin climbing a building. One other appearance of The Green Hornet, Kato, and Batman was broadcast in autumn 1966 on a Milton Berle Hollywood Palace television variety show.

JOHN NEGRON THE U.S.A. CONNECTION

I sat here wondering how I can come up with something interesting that a Bruce Lee fan as well as 1966 Green Hornet fans would enjoy.

After all I think after 50 years collecting I've just about read every article or story about my idol. Some stories true some made up others leaving thoughts to the imagination.

Well, after talking with Rick Baker on the phone I said how about something different. So all Bruce Lee fans are always interested in Pre-death articles or magazines on Bruce Lee and we all know these not only fetch high dollars but are very rare and hard to find. I started digging through my thousands of magazines and picked out some of the best ones for this Green Hornet issue. All were from magazine from 1966-67 articles that were written in the following magazines: Cracked, Mad, Not Brand Echh, (parody magazines), Sci-fi Mag's, and the following movie magazines Motion Picture, Movie Mirror, TV & Movie Screen, Photo play, TV radio show, Movie Life screen album, TV picture life, Movie land & TV time album, Newsweek, remember these magazines are 57 years old and the articles were published in them to publicize the coming of the Green Hornet to the TV screen. Van Williams who to be the Green Hornet was already a star in his own right for previous work but this was Bruce Lee's first big break, This was the first time as 6 year old that I got see Bruce Lee as Kato and I could not believe what I was seeing here this little guy was throwing guys around like rag dolls just a black blur to me but I was hooked on the campy Batman TV show but I watched the GH to see Kato. I did not know at the time that over 50 years later I would still be so amazed with this man named Bruce Lee! So sit back and enjoy this trip back down memory lane.

High in the Hollywood Hills, Van and Bruce can look through a telescope at the view. Van introduced Bruce to one of his favorite sports: motorcycling.

Boys will be boys. And sometimes men will be boys, too. When Van Williams and Bruce Lee, stars of ABC's **The Green Hornet**, took a day off from work, they decided to explore the Hollywood beaches and hills and ended up by acting like two kids just let out of school. However, the rough-and-tumble stuff on the beach is not as haphazard as it seems, for both Van and Bruce take their athletics very seriously. Van is an ex-football and track star as well as a former rodeo performer. He was born in Fort Worth, Texas on Feb. 27, 1934. His parents owned a large ranch there and, before Hollywood beckoned, Van intended to become a rancher. However, co-starring roles in four TV series, **Bourbon Street Beat, Surfside 6, Tycoon** and now **The Green Hornet,** have made his acting career secure. His private life is secure, too. He's been married to the former Vicki Richards since 1959 and they are the proud parents of four girls. The role of Kato on **The Green** (Continued on next page)

A day at the beach is just what the doctor ordered for two tired series stars. But do you think that they just lie around in the sun? Not these active guys!

Watching the episodes again, I can see Bruce Lee's star quality, even constrained by a chauffer's uniform, black mask and minimal dialogue. He moves like a cat, always hovering around the Hornet like some wicked guardian angel. In one episode, he had to resort to using the Hornet Sting to free his boss from a locked room. Where Van Williams usually opened the Sting like it was a telescope, Lee popped it open with a one-handed flourish that was sheer poetry. Williams must have thought it was the way to go because in subsequent episodes, he used his own variation of that particular bit of business.

Williams never copied Lee's Gung Fu moves, however. He settled for dukeing it out with assorted hoodlums and thugs. His fights usually paled beside Lee's, who went in for a lot of flashy kicks and leaps. Although Lee's mastery of the martial arts is beyond reproach, he freely admitted that Kato's fights were stylized for the camera.

"Some of the techniques used are not what I practice in Gung Fu," Lee explained. "For instance, I never believe in jumping and kicking. My kicks in actual Gung Fu are not high, but low, to the shin and the groin."

CASTING KATO

The story of how Bruce Lee obtained the role of Kato is interesting. Gung Fu had nothing to do with it. Lee, who was Cantonese, said that of all the Asian actors who tried out for the part, he caught the producer's attention because he was the only one who could pronounce the show's name without it coming out as *The Gleen Holnet*!

"It's a heck of a name," Lee said. "Every time I said it at that time, I was super conscious."

The supporting cast of **The Green Hornet** consisted of Wende Wagner, as Britt Reid's secretary Lenore "Casey" Case, and one of the few who knew his secret. Mike Axford, the *Sentinel*'s police reporter, did not have the privilege. He was played by character actor Lloyd Gough as an irrascible curmudgeon whose chief ambition in life was to capture the notorious Green Hornet. Both of those characters had been regulars on the old radio series.

District Attorney Frank Scanlon was not. He was the Hornet's unofficial police contact. Walter Brooke had the

PHOTO:
Bruce Lee as the trusty Kato, ready to deal with anyone that threatens law and order.

> *Casting Kato became a tricky affair. Bruce Lee only got the part because he could pronounce the name of his crimefighting partner. All the other Oriental actors kept calling him "The Gleen Holnet." Or, at least, that's how Lee remembered it!*

WHEN THE STARS COME OUT BY NIGHT

TIM O'CONNOR JIM DOUGLAS
This is what's known as keeping everything in the family—the "Peyton Place" family that is. Tim and Mary O'Connor make the evening a double header at the Cocoanut Grove with Dawn and Jim Douglas.

BRUCE LEE
Bruce and his charming wife, Linda spend an evening out on the town enjoying the company of good friends. Bruce is the champ as well as the author of a book on the sport of Gung Fu, and he stars as Kato in **The Green Hornet**.

DEBBIE REYNOLDS
Pert and as pretty as ever, Debbie Reynolds gives a staturesque pose to photog while hubby, Harry Karl looks on, delighted by his lovely young wife. Couple attended the Hollywood premiere of "Is Paris Burning?" which had its opening there last November.

Bruce Lee: LOVE KNOWS NO GEOGRAPHY

Bruce and Linda had to overcome many obstacles. But with faith in each other—and the human race—they proved their marriage could last!

The Lees—Bruce, Linda and Brandon Gok Ho—live in West Los Angeles. Though Brandon is only 20 months old, he is already showing an interest in his father's favorite sport of Gung Fu. Daddy is a champ on the subject, so Brandon can be assured of an expert's teaching.

■ How does it happen that two people from the opposite ends of the earth meet, fall in love, establish a true and contented union, and bring up their children as a triumph of human grace?

Let the story of Bruce Lee (Kato in 20th Century-Fox's *The Green Hornet*) and his wife, Linda Emery Lee, explain it.

Linda was born in Seattle, the younger of two sisters who were brought up in the Baptist faith. The Emerys are what the Hawaiians call "Haole" (Caucasian) or—as it is expressed colloquially, "garden-variety Americans."

After completing grade and high school in Seattle, Linda matriculated at the University of Washington with the intention of becoming a pediatrician.

Bruce Lee is also an American citizen, having been born in San Francisco. Bruce's beautiful Eurasian mother—one-fourth British, three-fourths Chinese—was touring with Bruce's father when the stork decided to deliver Bruce. The elder Mr. Lee—a famous Chinese opera singer—was appearing in San Francisco's Chinese Opera House at the time.

Bruce was the fourth child of a family to number five children; he has an elder brother and two elder sisters, plus one younger brother. When Bruce was three months old, the family returned to their Hong Kong home.

There Bruce was enrolled in a British private school where, as he says, he learned to pronounce "ox, fox and box" to rhyme with the American pronunciation of "hawks." Not by the remotest stretch of the imagination did Bruce Lee imagine he would ever marry and settle in the United States.

Once he had finished the equivalent of an American high school course, his family sent him to the University of Washington at Seattle, where he chose philosophy as his major. *(Please turn to page 50)*

BRUCE LEE:
"OUR MIXED MARRIAGE BROUGHT US A MIRACLE OF LOVE"

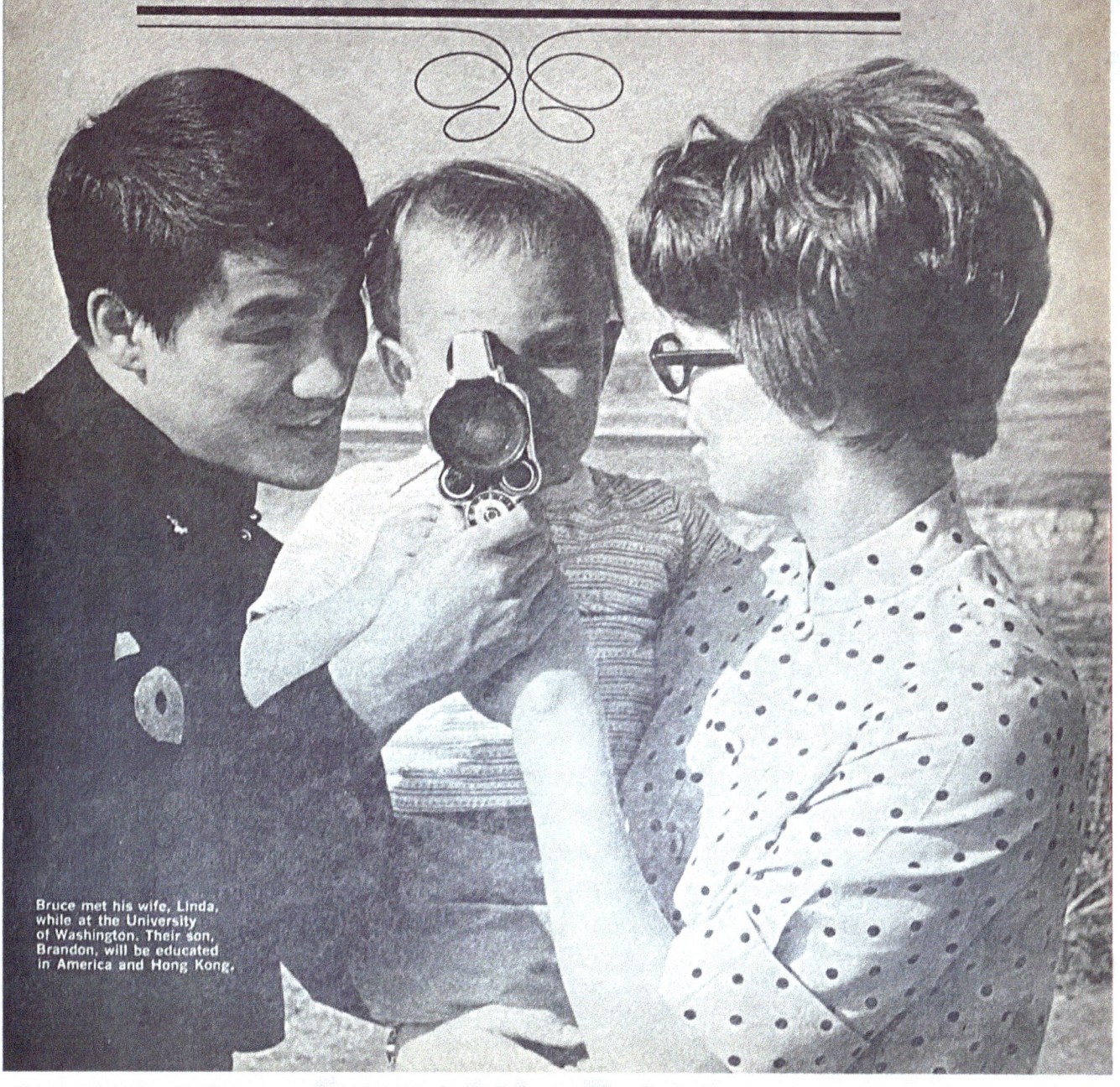

Bruce met his wife, Linda, while at the University of Washington. Their son, Brandon, will be educated in America and Hong Kong.

KUNG FU BONUS!

BRUCE LEE

Above: Linda Lee and her first child, Brendon, were pleased to pose for photos during the early days of Bruce's career. Right: A unique relationship exists between Bruce and Linda. He says she's more Oriental than a lot of the women he knew during his dating days back in China.

Affectionate father Bruce with son Brendon, who is now 8, shields his son and 4-year-old daughter Shannon from all publicity.

Even when Brendon was just a tot, Bruce began

36

MEET BRUCE LEE

THE GREEN HORNET'S BUZZ BOMB

And also meet Bruce's family; wife, Linda and son, Brandon.

Silhouetted against the sky are Linda, Bruce and Brandon, a happy family united in a moment of peace.

MEET KATO AND CREW

Danny Inosanto, who has a black belt in Karate, gets a taste of Gung Fu from his teacher, Bruce Lee.

Burt and Bonnie Ward live next door to Bruce Lee's family.

Newest crime fighter on the networks is also a devoted family man, a formidable athlete, and a relentless foe to his enemies.

The networks won't be safe for criminals when Brandon grows up!

ROBIN'S NEW LOVE RIVAL

Danny Inosanto and his wife Susan picnic with the Bruce Lees.

■ There is only one thing wrong with Bruce Lee--he's perfect! He's a perfect husband, a perfect father, and perfectly cast in the role of Kato, the faithful companion of the crime busting Britt Reid in ABC's *Green Hornet*. Robin, who has been *Batman's* side-kick, may find that Kato (Bruce) is a perfectly formidable rival.

Bruce is 145 perfect pounds, and is 5'8". He is 25 years old, born in the United States, but raised in Hong Kong. This is his first starring role, but he inherited his talent for show business from his father, who was a star of Chinese opera and used the name Lee Hoi Chuen. When Bruce was three years old, his family returned to Hong Kong, and he grew up among renowned singers and actors in the performing arts in China.

Because Bruce is dark, (*Please turn to page 63*)

39

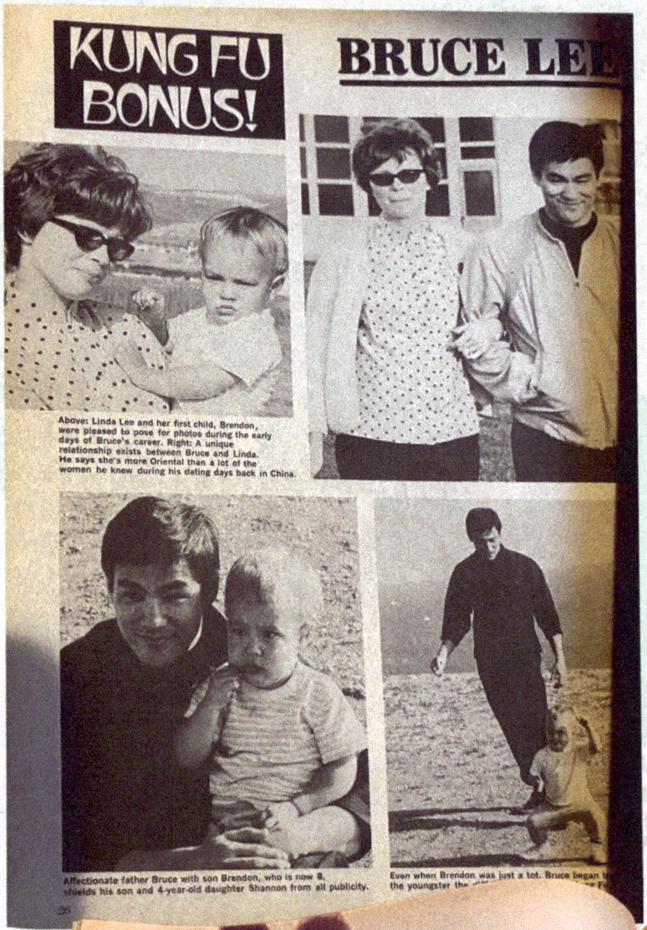

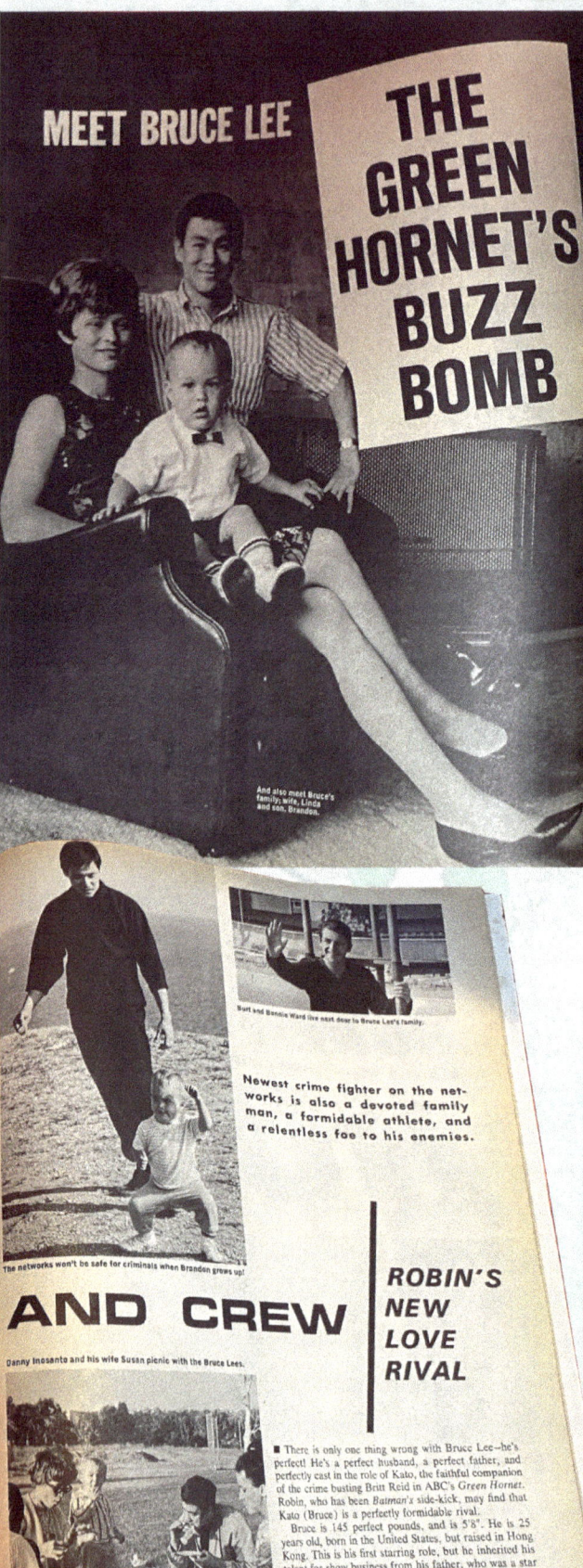

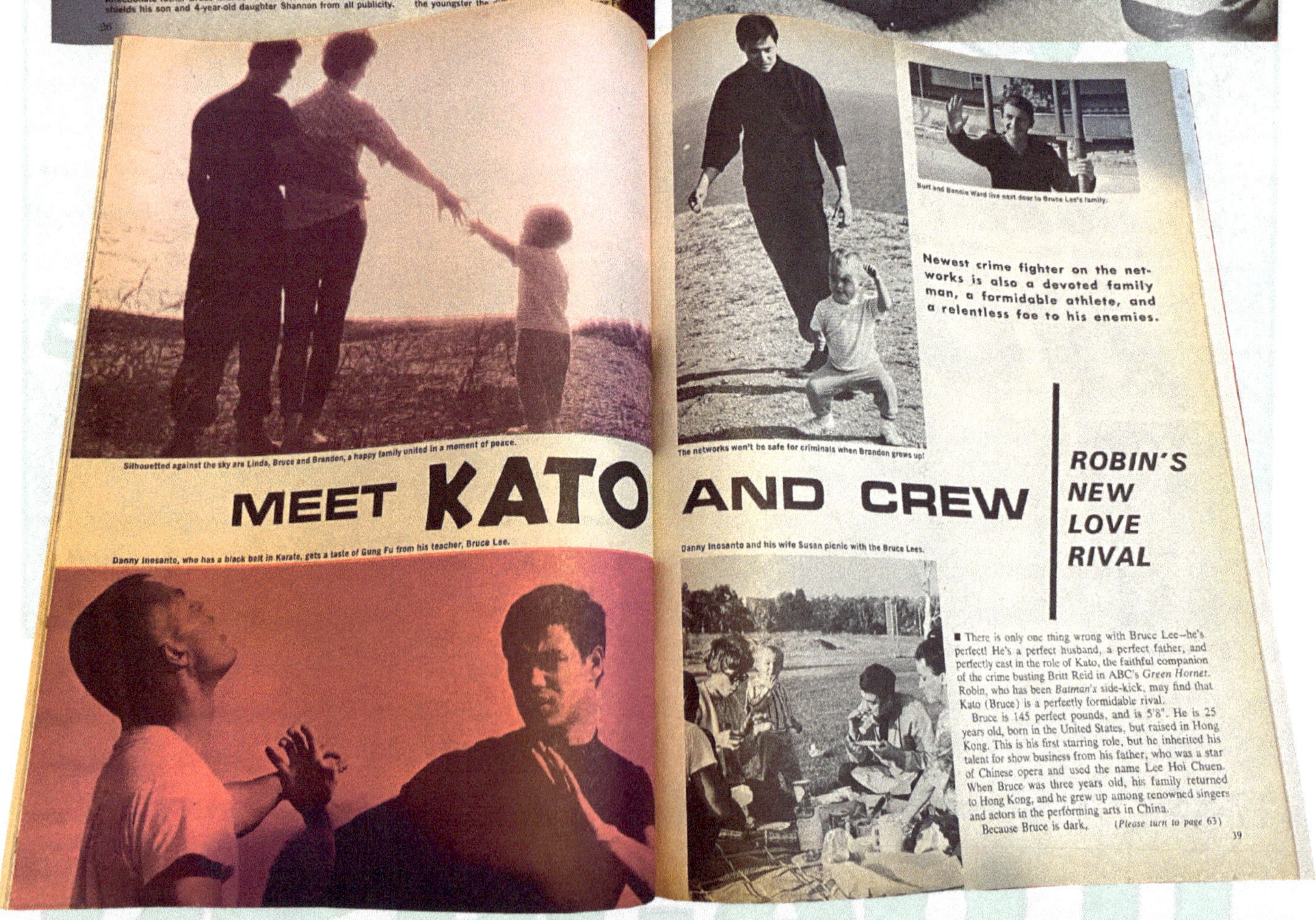

Who's the Green Hornet?

ONLY HIS SECRETARY KNOWS FOR SURE...

As the loyal right-hand (distaff side) of Britt Reed, alias The Green Hornet (enacted by Van Williams), Miss Case (played by Jynanne Wendy Wagner) keeps tabs on her boss' double-life and his feats of daring-do. To save his bothers she hits a classy fashion note in bright blouse of silhouette Navy (top above) from Casey in costume at Alexander wool crepe. Bringing her day a night in a stylish and...

Presenting Linda, Brandon and Bruce Lee.

What It's REALLY Like To Live A MIXED MARRIAGE!

Mrs. Bruce Lee, strawberry-blonde wife of the handsome Chinese actor who plays Kato on <u>The Green Hornet</u>, doesn't need the ancient Oriental art of Gung Fu to defend herself and her family

■ When little Brandon Lee starts school in a few years, he'll probably be the only child in his class proficient in Gung Fu, that ancient Oriental art which spawned Karate. His daddy—known to video viewers as *The Green Hornet*'s inventive valet Kato—is also a professional Gung Fu instructor, and from the time he could toddle, Brandon got lessons in this artful form of self-defense.

Now Brandon will undoubtedly be involved in more than the active youngster's share of skirmishes—for the simple reason that he is the child of a racially mixed marriage.

Bruce Lee, 25, who grew up in Hong Kong, is a slight, sinewy young man with a kinetic smile and a gregarious nature. His wife Linda, 21, is a native of Seattle who fits the / *please turn to page 77*

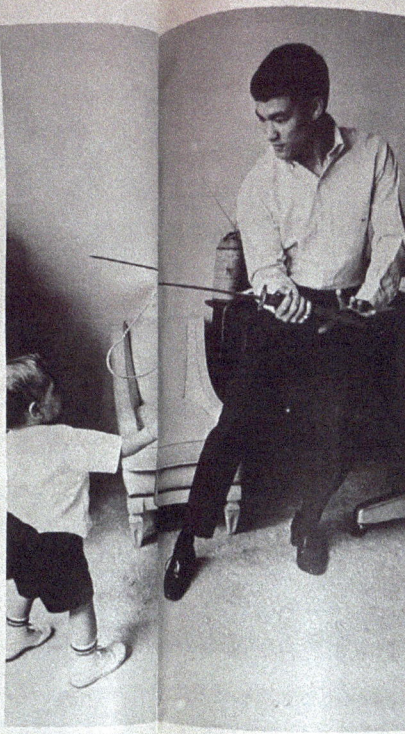

No rattles or blocks for Brandon! As a toddler this sturdy boy was taught Gung Fu by expert dad.

Combining the wisdom of the East, the informality of the West, the Lees have created a life that is the best of both worlds.

TV Stars who'll turn you on...

Above: Holy hornets, will you be seeing more of this duo! That's Bruce Lee at the left and Van Williams to the right. Who are, in case you haven't guessed, the stars of the new "Green Hornet" series. Below: The men from you-know-where (Vaughn & McCallum), here with U.N.C.L.E. chief Leo G. Carroll, will be back with their series, also on the Girl-from-same show. You'll also go ape for the first TV "Tarzan", muscle-man Ron Ely, who should sure help the season swing!

TV Preview: THE MAN TO WATCH
Van Williams: The Lowdown on The Green Hornet

By William Colbert

Hollywood is buzzing over the handsome Hornet—and here's why you will, too!

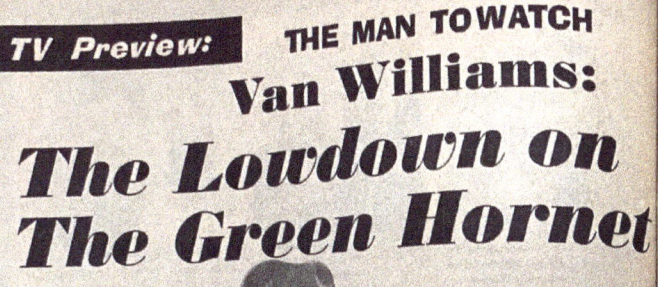

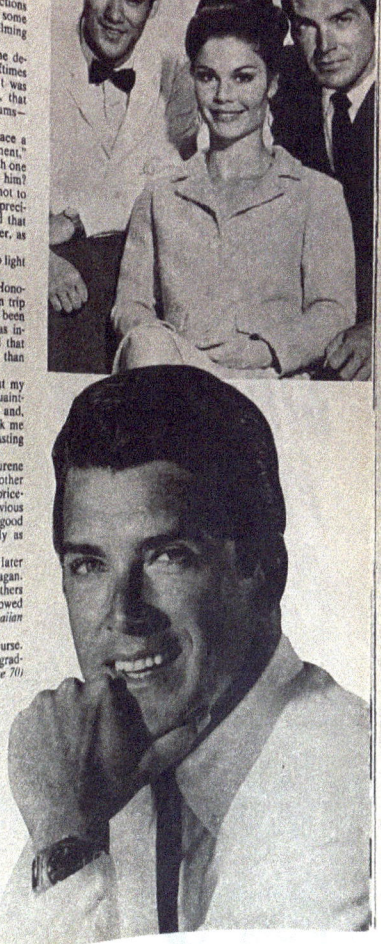

"The Green Hornet set was buzzing with excitement. Photographers, reporters and gossip columnists were everywhere. There was some difficulty in organization since it was only the first day of shooting, and everyone seemed to be running in a dozen different directions at the same time. Finally, though, after a while, some semblance of calm was established, and the filming began."

These are the words of Wende Wagner as she described her initial exposure to the exciting, oftimes chaotic world of television series production. It was obvious, during our recent exclusive interview, that Wende found the experience—and Van Williams—unforgettable.

"My first meeting with Van actually took place a week before we shot the first Green Hornet segment," she told me. "We did a photo session together with one of the local photographers. My impression of him? Well, I found him to be an extremely nice guy, not to mention very good-looking, with a wonderful appreciation of the outdoors-kind-of-life. We discovered that we had a great deal in common with one another, as I also like to play tennis, swim and surf."

If a little research is done, certain facts come to light that show how remarkably alike they are.

For one thing, they both spent many months in Honolulu. Van went there on a post-graduate vacation trip from Texas Christian University where he had been an agriculture major. While in Honolulu, he was introduced to the late Mike Todd who suggested that Van try acting, instead of farming. So, rather than head back for Texas, he went to Hollywood.

"I found the film capital singularly blase about my arrival," he said recently. "I had only a few acquaintances in town, no family connections to help me and, worst of all, no show business experience to back me up when I started making the rounds of the casting offices.

"However, at a party one evening, I met Lurene Tuttle who was then appearing in the role of Mother in Life With Father. She gave me one word of priceless advice: 'Study!' That may seem trite and obvious but I heeded the suggestion, signed on with a good dramatic coach, and applied myself as intensely as humanly possible."

Van's first professional break came months later when he was cast in a telefilm with Ronald Reagan. This exposure led to a contract with Warner Brothers and a regular role on Bourbon Street Beat, followed by Surfside 6, and guest appearances on Hawaiian Eye, 77 Sunset Strip and Gallant Men.

Wende's career followed much the same course. She, too, went on a vacation to Honolulu after graduating from high school *(Continued on page 70)*

Rumor says this may be the hottest trio since the Andrews Sisters. Bruce Lee plays Kato, Wende Wagner gets around as the pretty secretary, and Van Williams simply tears around as the G.H. Not surprisingly, rumor-mongers in Hollywood are trying to hint a romance between Van and Wende—it's pretty obvious why—but she says they're just friends, and he's a happily married man, so everybody ought to lay off. Ha!

Shown here is an original pack of SEALED gum Cards with Box & a sticker pack with box from 1966 with a few cards from each to show what they looked like. These are very special to me as the cards & stickers were survivors from when I bought them as a kid. The reason I still have some of my original GH toys is when I was a kid, I would ask for Batman toys and would get GH ones so I would throw them in a box because I wasn't really interested in those they weren't as cool and flashy as the Batman ones at the time. Who would have known that these toys would become so valuable because of their limited availability and production. most of the toys upon coming out was after the show had been cancelled due to only one season of air time.

Shown here is a VERY RARE 1966 Sheet music program. The reason this program is so rare is because of the Green Border very difficult to find in Mint condition due to the border getting badly damaged when handled and also a very limited print just available at Music specialty shops that carried sheet music. How many GH fans went into those??? Also shown is the rare soundtrack by Al Hirt (My favorite album cover of the few different ones produced) this one was signed at Van Williams very first convention appearance since he left on the GH series.

April 1993 • TOY SHOP •

ORIGINAL GREEN HORNET " BLACK BEAUTY " FIRST TIME ON DISPLAY Courtesy of J. R. Goodman

Shown here are some my personal Autographs from the main characters of the 1966 Green Hornet series.

Van Williams as the Green Hornet, Wende Wagner as Ms. Case and also shown is my original 1967 signed Gas receipt by Bruce Lee (quick note look how much Bruce Lee paid for 10 Gallons of Gas in 1967 just over $3 USD!!)

BRUCE LEE
•

Arthur Kennard Associates, Inc.
OL-2-6750

VAN WILLIAMS
•

William Morris Agency, Inc.
CR-4-7451   BR-2-4111

Shown here is a 1966 Advertising agency cards for Van Williams & Bruce Lee. I'm guessing these were given to Hollywood agents for studios to reference their clients to hire them for parts.

RARE 1966 photo of Bruce on the Beach during publicity photo shoots with Co-star Van Williams (not Shown in photo)

Here comes the Green Hornet's "BLACK BEAUTY"
"FASTER, KATO!"
The Official Hobby Kit by Aurora!
98¢
AURORA

Here comes the Green Hornet's "BLACK BEAUTY"
"FASTER, KATO!"
The Official Hobby Kit by Aurora!
98¢
AURORA

Here comes the Green Hornet's "BLACK BEAUTY"
"FASTER, KATO!"
The Official Hobby Kit by Aurora!

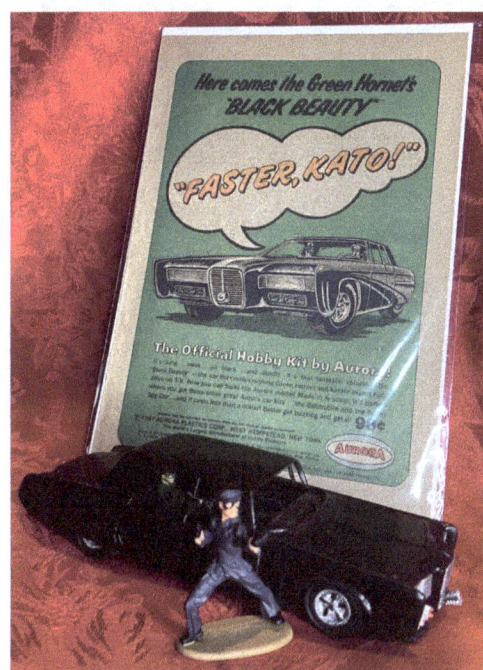

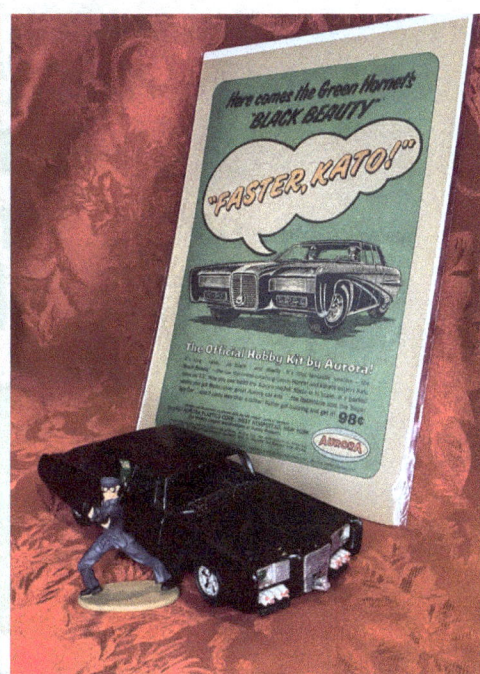

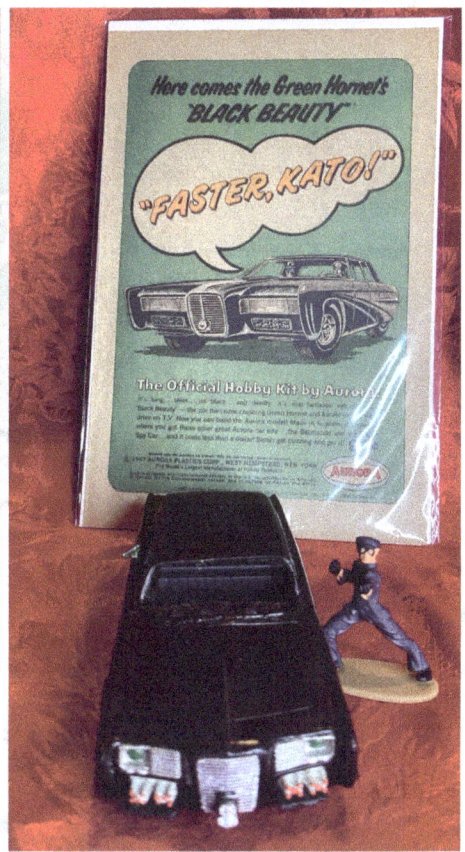

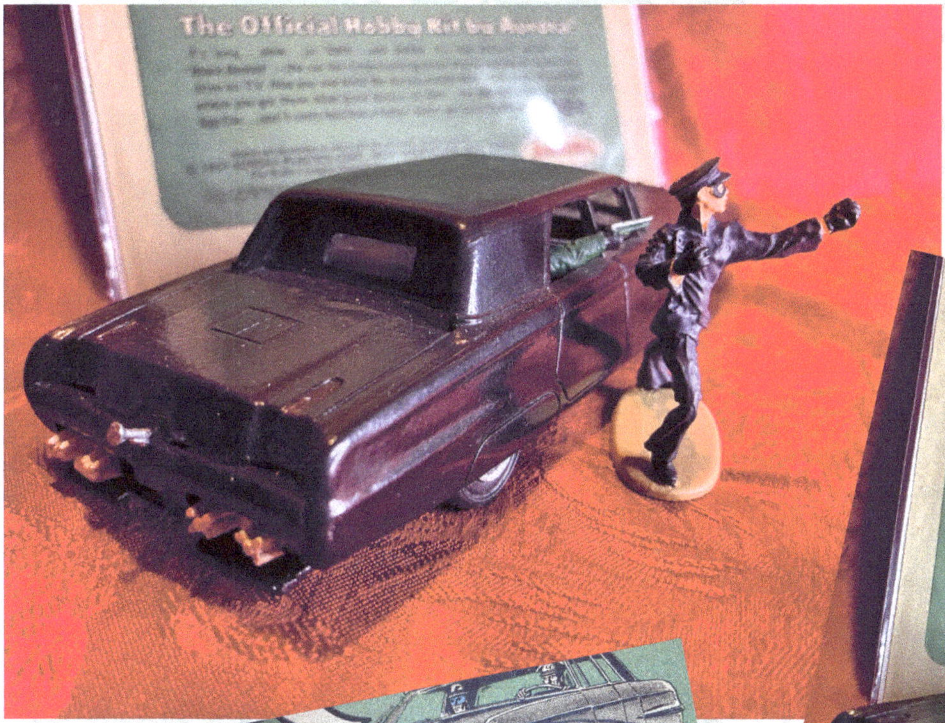
The Official Hobby Kit by Aurora

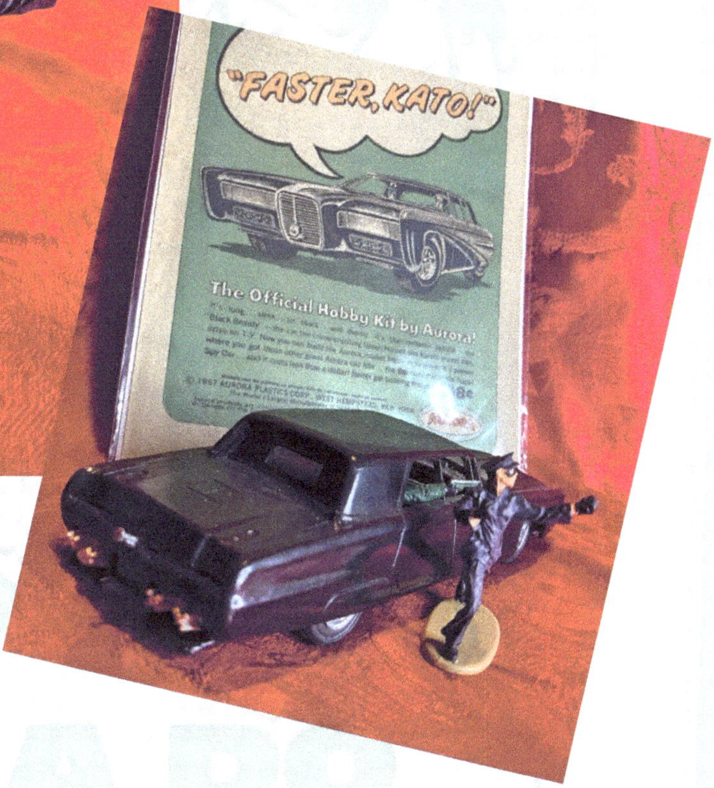
"FASTER, KATO!"
The Official Hobby Kit by Aurora!

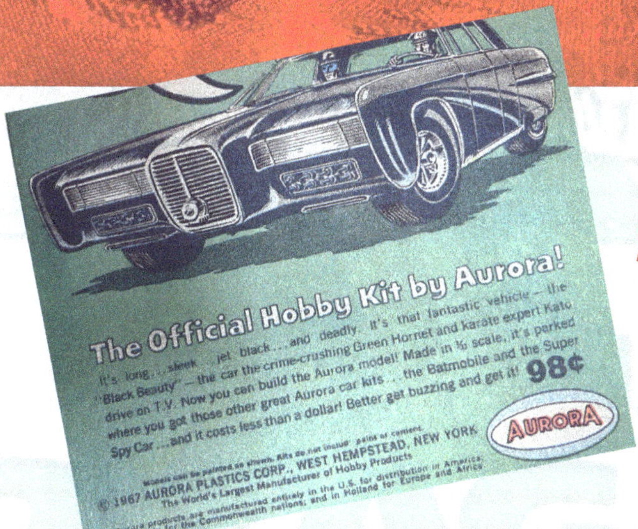
The Official Hobby Kit by Aurora!
It's long... sleek... jet black... and deadly. It's that fantastic vehicle – the "Black Beauty" – the car the crime-crushing Green Hornet and karate expert Kato drive on T.V. Now you can build the Aurora model! Made in ⅛ scale, it's parked where you got those other great Aurora car kits... the Batmobile and the Super Spy Car ... and it costs less than a dollar! Better get buzzing and get it!
98¢
AURORA
© 1967 AURORA PLASTICS CORP., WEST HEMPSTEAD, NEW YORK
The World's Largest Manufacturer of Hobby Products
Aurora products are manufactured entirely in the U.S. for distribution in America; in Canada for the Commonwealth nations; and in Holland for Europe and Africa.

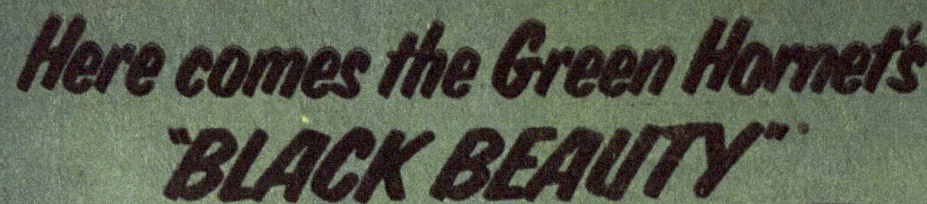

GREEN HORNET FANS!!!

RECOGNIZE THIS CAR?????

1ST NEW PICTURES THE BLACK BEAUTY

I have documentation showing Fox TV as owner in 1967. The car is currently being restored by Dean Jeffries exactly as it appeared on Green Hornet. Car runs excellent. Serious bids of $500,000 or highest bid will be accepted. This is the best item to add to any Green Hornet Collection.

I John Negron would like to dedicate this GH section to the Late J.R Goodman, Although I never met him in person, I met J.R in the 90's through a posting that he did in a collector's newspaper when he was buying the Original Black Beauty to have it restored. We became pen pals and at that time there wasn't a whole lot of footage out there of the GH show except really bad generation copies, But J.R being the great guy and GH fan that he was would send me footage at the time that only he had such as behind the scenes footage, unedited shows, commercials, ads and more. We exchanged photos and footage for years.... To make a long story short just recently J.R lost his battle with Cancer, he will be missed as he was always one to share his collection with others. Although he is gone, he will not be forgotten. Rest easy and in Peace, The world of GH collectors has lost a very true and dedicated fan and someone I was proud to call a true friend.

John Negron

Thank you's

Compiled & edited by Rick Baker

Tim Hollingsworth
(Cover Design & iterior layour)

Mike Nesbitt
Chris Poggiali
Special Thank to
John Negron
Thomas Gross

Special thanks to Mihn Loung for the restoration of the cover image of Bruce Lee

www.ingramcontent.com/pod-product-compliance
Lightning Source LLC
Chambersburg PA
CBHW051323110526
44590CB00031B/4454